Building *Your Own* Kitchen Cabinets

Building Your Own Kitchen Cabinets

Layout · Materials · Construction · Installation

Jere Cary

The Taunton Press

Fourth printing: April 1986
International Standard Book Number 0-918804-15-9
Library of Congress Catalog Card Number 82-051260
Printed in the United States of America

A FINE WOODWORKING Book

FINE WOODWORKING® is a trademark of The Taunton Press, Inc.,
registered in the U.S. Patent and Trademark Office.

The Taunton Press, Inc.
63 South Main Street
Box 355
Newtown, Connecticut 06470

My wife, Gretta, has shared in the excitement of this project from the start. She has been my sounding board, typist and proofreader, and has provided encouragement and understanding every step of the way. To her I lovingly dedicate this book.

Contents

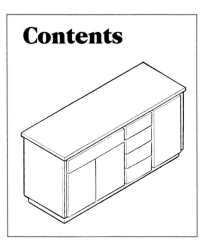

Acknowledgments

Without the encouragement and help of many friends, students and family members, this book could not have come into existence. I especially wish to thank:

Sixten "Sag" Anderson, a master craftsman and teacher, for teaching me machine and hand-tool skills, the tricks of the trade and pride in a job well done. He has been my woodworking consultant and an inspiration for many years.

Patti Polinsky Claar, for giving me the nudge that set the typewriter in motion, and for her field-testing of this work.

Bill Sorensen, for his ideas and answers, and for the many good woodworking conversations we've had in his cabinet shop.

Bob Lakey, for his expertise and help with the chapter on finishing.

Introduction

Most of us can look back over the years and pick out a few events that were extremely important in shaping our lives. At the time the event occurred, it may not have seemed too important, but years of hindsight show it to be a major fork in life's road. There have been two such events in my life. One happened nearly 30 years ago, when I was only two years out of college and about to be married. With too many demands on my beginning salary, and in need of furniture to appropriately furnish an apartment for a new wife, I sought out a friend, Sixten "Sag" Anderson, a Swedish cabinetmaker. My woodworking attempts had been disastrous up to this point, and so I went to Sag for advice and help. Fortunately for me, Sag was more than a master cabinetmaker, he was a master teacher. Oh, not in the formal sense of the word, but he knew when to encourage, when to criticize, how to explain, and when to throw down his cap. His influence on me was great. In a matter of four years, I'd gone from building an apartment full of furniture to building a home. Then I returned to college for a degree in industrial-arts education, so that I could teach others what Sag taught me.

During the early part of my teaching career, it was only natural that I search for a book to explain the details of the cabinetmaking process. When I couldn't find one, I developed some materials to hand out to students, to supplement the class demonstrations. The second important event happened when I returned to class after an illness, and a student in one of my community-college classes, Patti Polinsky Claar, suggested that the handouts be expanded into a book so students might carry on their work in spite of my health. The wheels started to turn, and I began work on this book.

I wrote with the hope that the book would serve as a shop tool for the beginner, and a resource for craftsmen at all levels. Therefore, the skeleton of the text is the plan of procedure for laying out and building a cabinet. A plan of procedure may be described as a list of steps, in their proper order, necessary to complete a complex task. The skeleton is padded with background information, principles and tricks of the trade. (The plan of procedure, in its simplest form, may be found in Appendix 3. More detailed parts of it can be found and identified in each chapter as numbered steps.)

When the book was finished, I realized that bits of information taken out of the total context of cabinetmaking could cause great confusion and perhaps even ruin the project. For that reason, it is important that readers at least skim all the chapters before making any wood shavings. It is also critical that readers have had instruction, either by book or in a class, in the safe operation of power tools before beginning the work. (The bibliography on p. 138 lists several good books that cover power tools.)

Students enter my high-school and community-college classes with a wide range of woodworking experiences behind them. But important as it may seem, previous experience alone is not the best guarantee of future success. In my years of teaching, I have found that desire to do the job, appreciation for accuracy, good organization, and the ability to follow directions are the characteristics of the most successful cabinetmakers.

May your story sticks be accurate,
Your saw cut true,
And may the pleasures of cabinetmaking
Come to you.

Jere Cary
January 1983

Cabinets and Kitchens

Chapter 1

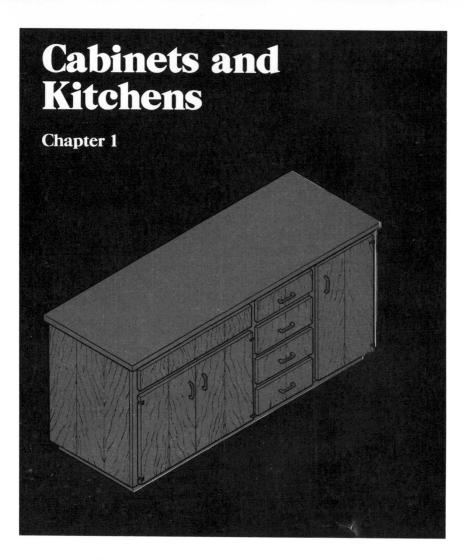

A kitchen cabinet, in its simplest form, is not much more than a box. It has a top, bottom, back and ends. The back and a 2½-in. to 4-in.-wide nail rail together hold the cabinet square and prevent it from racking side to side. The inside space of a cabinet can be divided by partitions and shelves or drawers, or by variations such as pull-out trays or lazy Susans. The front of the cabinet is covered by a face frame made of solid wood, which hides the raw edges of the plywood used for the ends, bottom and partitions. (The vertical members of the face frame are called stiles; the horizontal members, rails.) The face frame extends beyond the cabinet by about ¼ in. to allow for fitting the cabinet tight to an uneven wall. The whole cabinet is supported 4 in. above the floor on a separate frame called a toeboard; the toeboard, set back 3 in. from the front of the cabinet, allows space for the user's toes.

Most kitchen cabinets are built to standard heights and depths, as shown in the drawing on the opposite page. Widths are arbitrary, depending on the shape of the kitchen and the special needs of its user. Altering standard dimensions should only be done after considering the consequences. For example, changing the standard counter height of 36 in. to accommodate a person shorter or taller than average may make it difficult to sell the house later to someone of average height. You may also have trouble installing appliances because some floor-model stoves, built-in dishwashers and trash compactors are designed for the standard height. (Of course, you could substitute a drop-in range and built-in oven for the floor model, or install the appliance under a standard-height counter and change the other counters to suit.)

Many people like to have a desk in their kitchen. To be comfortable, a desktop should be about 12 in. higher than the chair seat—about 30 in. from the floor, with an average-height chair. But if the desk is to be an extension of a 36-in.-high countertop, the user will need a 24-in.-high stool. The width of the kneehole, the open space under the desk, is determined by the width of the chair; kneeholes of 20 in. to 22 in. are usually adequate.

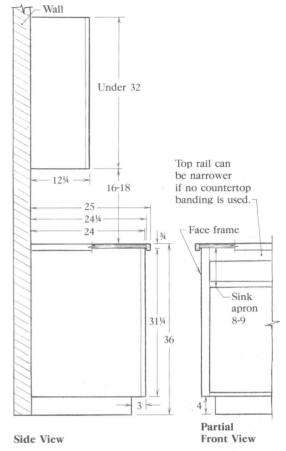

Side View

Partial Front View

Here are some standard kitchen-cabinet heights and depths; widths depend on the shape of the kitchen and user needs. Bathroom vanities are usually about 32 in. tall (including the toeboard) and 20 in. to 24 in. deep.

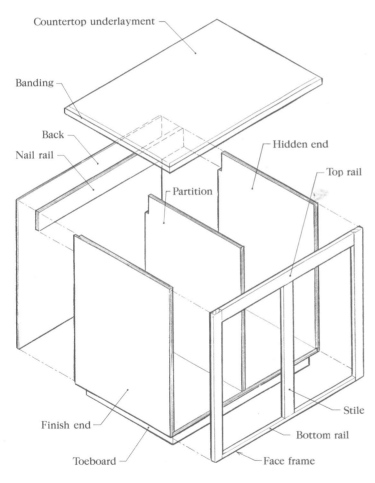

A cabinet is basically a box, held square by the back and nail rail. The toeboard lets the user stand close, and the face frame hides the edges of the ends, bottom and partitions.

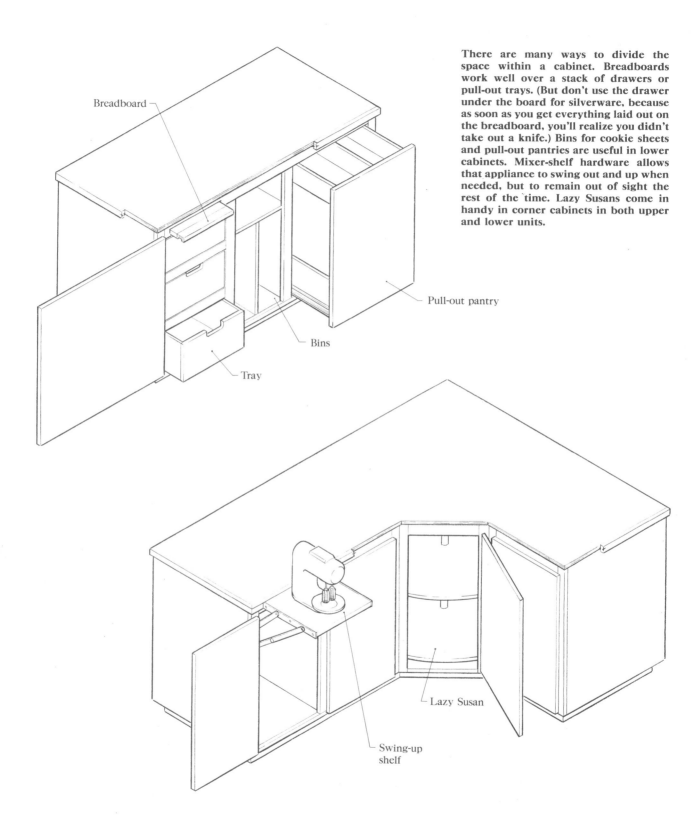

There are many ways to divide the space within a cabinet. Breadboards work well over a stack of drawers or pull-out trays. (But don't use the drawer under the board for silverware, because as soon as you get everything laid out on the breadboard, you'll realize you didn't take out a knife.) Bins for cookie sheets and pull-out pantries are useful in lower cabinets. Mixer-shelf hardware allows that appliance to swing out and up when needed, but to remain out of sight the rest of the time. Lazy Susans come in handy in corner cabinets in both upper and lower units.

Breadboard

Pull-out pantry

Bins

Tray

Swing-up shelf

Lazy Susan

Cabinet Styles

The appearance of a kitchen cabinet depends on its door and drawer faces. There are three basic styles of cabinet faces: lip, flush and overlay.

A lip face is larger than the door or drawer opening; its rabbeted edges cover a little of the face frame. Cabinets with lip faces are the easiest to build because they are somewhat forgiving: doors and drawers can be fitted correctly despite slight errors in size or squareness.

Flush faces are set flush with the face frame. It takes great skill to fit the faces into the frame with an even margin of clearance on all sides.

An overlay face is also larger than its opening, but its edges aren't rabbeted—the total thickness of the door or drawer sits on the top of the face frame. Overlay faces may also be used without a face frame, or with a partial face frame. You must fit the faces very closely if using a partial face frame or if omitting the face frame entirely—inaccuracies are difficult, if not impossible, to hide.

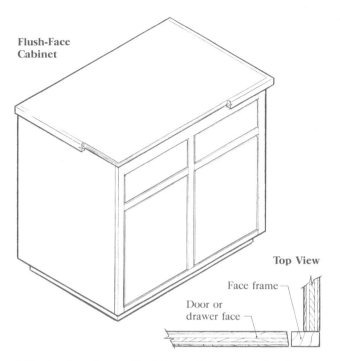

Flush-Face Cabinet

Top View

Face frame

Door or drawer face

This drawing shows a flush-face cabinet with a face frame, but you can make one with a partial face frame, too.

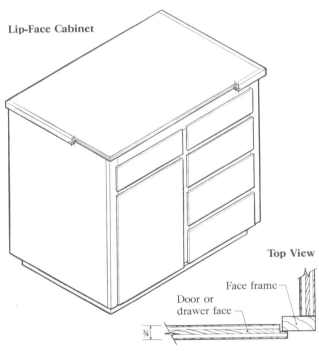

Lip-Face Cabinet

Top View

Face frame

Door or drawer face

¾

Lip faces for doors and drawers have rabbeted edges that cover a bit of the face frame.

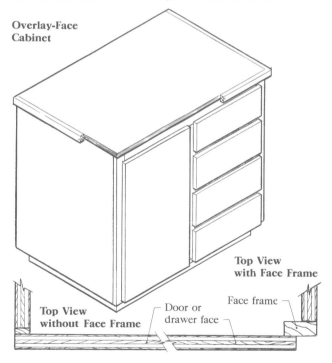

Overlay-Face Cabinet

Top View with Face Frame

Face frame

Top View without Face Frame

Door or drawer face

Overlay faces lie on the top of the face frame. These faces can be used without a face frame (detail at left), or with just the vertical members (stiles) of the frame.

Door and drawer faces can be as decorative as you wish. You can make them from hardwood plywood with intriguing grain, or from solid wood using frame-and-panel construction. Plywood faces can be decorated with homemade or commercial edge molding or appliqué molding. You can machine detail on a plywood face with a router and template, or simply rout grooves parallel to the edges of the door or drawer faces as decoration.

Door and drawer faces made from solid wood add a feeling of richness to a kitchen, but you pay for it in materials and labor. Putting raised panels in frames (p. 64) is one way to build attractive, solid-wood faces. Because wood shrinks and swells across the grain with changes in humidity, the panel should not be glued into the frame, so that it can move freely with seasonal changes. Plywood can also be used for the panel of a frame-and-panel door or drawer, and plywood won't shrink or swell, so it can be glued in place. If you use thin plywood (¼ in. to ½ in. thick), you can make the grooves in the rails and the stiles as wide as the plywood is thick. Edge molding, appliqué and sawn or routed detail can all be used on frame-and-panel faces.

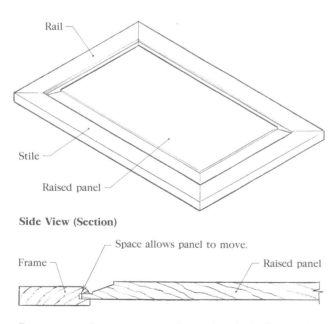

Side View (Section)

Because wood moves across the grain, don't fit a solid-wood panel into its frame tightly.

The Kitchen

A kitchen is more than a collection of cabinets—it's greater than the sum of its parts. How much greater depends on the way the elements are arranged. The gourmet cook will obviously have different requirements than the hurried executive who cooks out of cans. A candymaker will need a place to store specialized utensils and a marble countertop on which to cool the candy. A baker will need extra storage space for flour and sweeteners. Though I can teach how to lay out and build a kitchen full of cabinets, I can't give a recipe for the perfect kitchen. The details of each one will be as individual as its user. It is the cabinetmaker's responsibility to find out the needs of the person who will be using the kitchen, and then to accommodate those needs, considering principles of economy and the structure of the room.

Here, however, are some general guidelines to aid in the placement of cabinets within the kitchen. The recommendations for each work center, given in linear feet, are thought by home economists to be the most efficient, but don't worry if you can't follow them exactly. The centers aren't all used at once, so sometimes one center can perform two functions. (To make two work centers into one, just add 1 ft. to the widest of the two counter dimensions.)

The refrigerator center doesn't require cabinets, but there should be 2½ ft. to 3 ft. of counter space between the refrigerator and sink. The refrigerator door should hinge on the side away from the counter.

The preferred location of the mixing center is between the refrigerator and the sink. The center should have 3 ft. to 5 ft. of counter space; lower and upper cabinets should provide storage for dry ingredients, baking pans and small appliances. Electrical outlets are needed in this center.

The cooking center has changed considerably within recent years. It used to have just an oven and range top, but now the center can have a microwave oven and a number of other specialized cooking appliances. Pay attention to storage area for all these items, as well as for the usual cooking utensils; leave about 3½ ft. to 5 ft. of open counter space to be covered with a heat-resistant material, such as plastic laminate. Seasonings are often needed in the cooking center, so consider providing a place for them. Drawers always come in handy for storing stirring, turning and testing utensils.

The serving center is usually located between the stove and dining area. About 2 ft. of counter space is enough. Cabinets in this center will hold condiments, serving dishes and trays, and possibly linens, place-mats and napkins.

The sink center is where most kitchen time is spent. The sink is usually centered under a window, with the dishwasher to the left. About 2½ ft. to 3 ft. of counter space on each side of the sink is adequate. Upper cabinets for dishes should be placed over the dishwasher or close to it. The cabinets on the other side of the sink should store foods that need soaking, washing or water for their preparation.

When laying out the size and placement of work centers, keep in mind that work is usually done from right to left. That is, food from the refrigerator moves left to the mixing center or sink and then left to the stove. After rinsing at the sink, the dishes

move left to the dishwasher and then move up or to the left into the cabinets.

A line drawn from the center of the refrigerator, to the center of the sink, to the center of the cooking center and back to the refrigerator marks what is called the work triangle. Ideally, the perimeter of this triangle should be between 13 ft. and 22 ft. A work triangle less than 13 ft. probably means the kitchen is cramped; over 22 ft. means that the user will waste steps in moving from center to center.

There are several basic kitchen shapes that the cabinetmaker will encounter.

The U-shaped kitchen, shown in the drawing below, is one of the most efficient kitchens. With the proper arrangement of appliances, counters and cabinets, steps can be reduced to a minimum and kitchen work made much easier for the user. One advantage of U-shaped kitchens, which is not provided by the kitchens shown on the following page, is that traffic through the work area is practically eliminated.

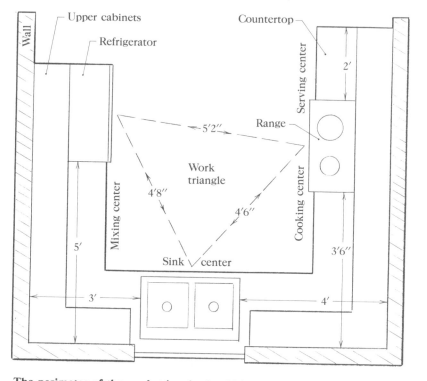

The perimeter of the work triangle should be no larger than 22 ft. and no smaller than 13 ft.

The strip kitchen is simply a long, narrow space with the cabinets arranged in a straight line along one wall. This type of kitchen usually has an entrance at both ends. Because of the resulting traffic, and because more steps are required to accomplish any given task, the strip kitchen is the least efficient kitchen design.

A variation of the strip kitchen is the Pullman kitchen. It, too, is a narrow passageway, but is wide enough to have cabinets on both walls, so you can store twice as much as in a strip kitchen. Traffic may still be a problem, but the extra cabinet space and compactness of this layout makes this kitchen more efficient than the strip kitchen.

The *L*-shaped kitchen may not be quite as efficient as the Pullman kitchen or the *U*-shaped kitchen, but it is quite acceptable to work in and there are no serious traffic problems.

Large or open kitchens can be made more efficient if a peninsula unit or an island unit is added. These cabinets not only help route traffic, they can be used to separate the kitchen and dining areas, too.

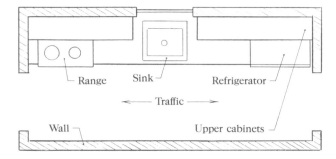

A strip kitchen is the least efficient design. If the kitchen is wide enough to add cabinets and appliances to the opposite wall (resulting in a Pullman kitchen), as shown at right, the efficiency of the room is considerably improved.

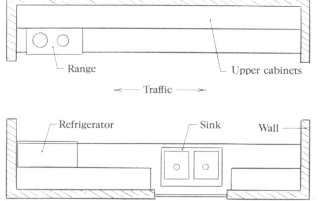

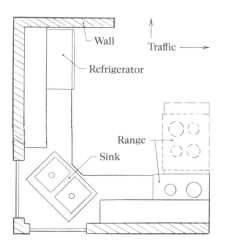

L-shaped kitchens are not as efficient as U-shaped ones, but are better than strip kitchens. A peninsula added to this kitchen would help control traffic, as well as separate the kitchen from the dining area.

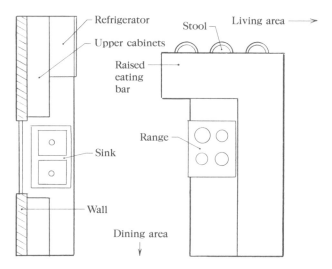

In houses with open floor plans, an island unit is a popular way to divide the cooking and living areas.

Cabinet Breakdown

Though the cabinets work together in the kitchen, they must be made separately. When figuring out the type and placement of the cabinets, plan where they should be broken into separate units for ease in construction, transportation and installation.

Several factors influence the size of each unit. Most plywood comes in sheets that are 96 in. long, and although long cabinets aren't impossible to build, it may be a problem to join the bottom, top and back. Long, heavy cabinets can be awkward to handle and install, too. Consider how you will transport the cabinets to the kitchen, and the dimensions of the doors and halls the cabinets must pass through.

If the breakdown is handled correctly, the joints between cabinets won't show. A good place to join two units is at a corner, or at a tall unit like an oven cabinet, pantry or broom closet. If the face frames of the two cabinets are flush, it will be hard to get a good joint between them, so make one unit 1 in. deeper than the other.

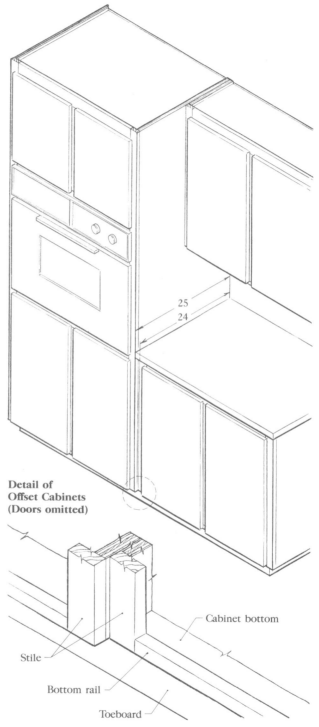

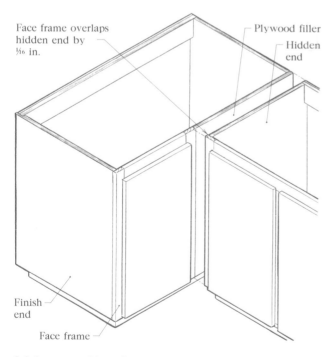

Joining two cabinets in a corner is an excellent way to hide the seam.

When two cabinets join side to side, make one of them about 1 in. deeper for a tight, neat joint.

If the job requires a long, straight run of cabinets, several construction solutions are possible. You can build and install individual cabinets and cover them all with one face frame. Or, you can emphasize the joints by eliminating the rails in the face frame. In this case, each cabinet is built with a stile on only one side, but the stile is wide enough to cover the end of the adjoining cabinet.

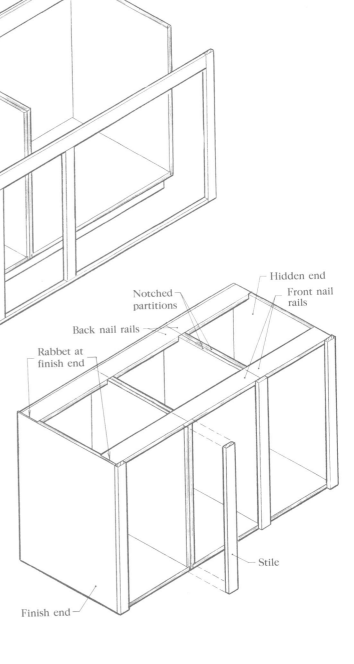

One face frame, attached to a long row of cabinets that are individually built and installed, can make the cabinets appear to be one unit.

Emphasize the places where cabinets join by building each cabinet with only one stile. The face-up nail rails also allow prelaminated countertops to be screwed on.

Hidden end

Front nail rails

Notched partitions

Back nail rails

Rabbet at finish end

Stile

Finish end

Another way to emphasize the individual units is to build a series of cabinets, each with its own face frame, then install the cabinets with a recessed stile between them.

Cabinetmakers must also think about function and installation when deciding how to break down a job into units. The cabinets shown in the drawing below will look the same when they're installed, but notice the difference in usable shelf space. A difficult installation can often be simplified by rearranging the units, as shown in the drawing below at right.

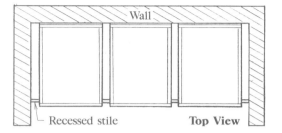

You can also build a series of cabinets with individual face frames, and then install recessed stiles between them.

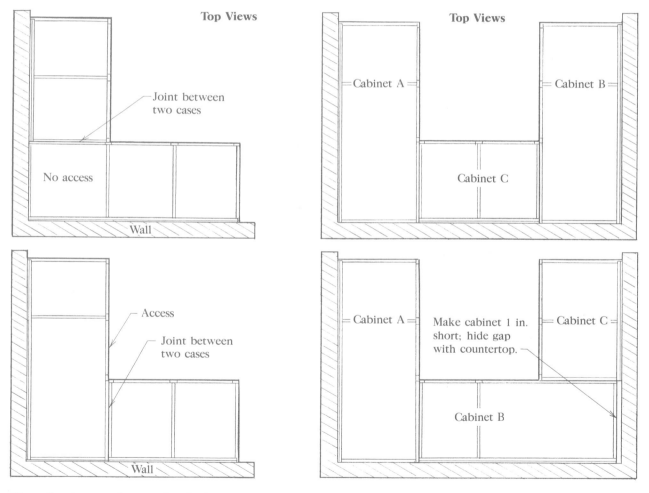

When figuring out how to break down the cabinets in a job, beware of creating the kind of useless space found in the cabinet shown in the top drawing.

In the top drawing, cabinets A and B must be put in first, and cabinet C slid or dropped into place, at the risk of damaged faces and poor fit. Cabinets broken down as shown in the bottom drawing slip easily into place.

Story Sticks

Chapter 2

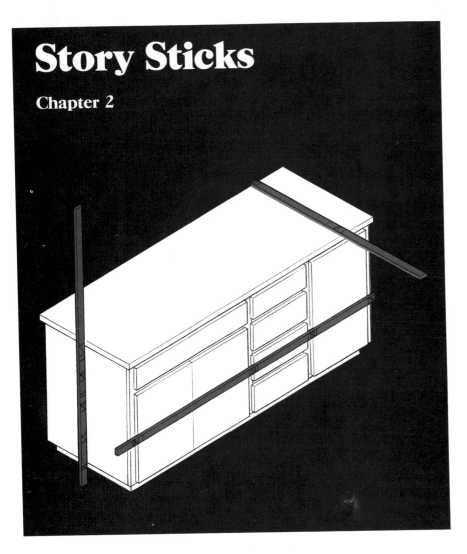

Story sticks are one of the kitchen cabinetmaker's most valuable tools: on these long, narrow pieces of wood, an entire kitchenful of cabinets can be laid out full size. The positions of the doors and windows, electrical and plumbing services, and other details are recorded on the sticks first. Then the details of the cabinets and the fixed appliances in each work center are added. Because all the cabinet parts and joints are marked out full size, it's easier and more accurate to build from story sticks than from small-scale drawings.

Using the sticks may seem awkward at first, but I often find that even people who are apprehensive when they start come to rely heavily on story sticks once they have seen how much help the sticks can

be. For example, the room details on the sticks let you determine exactly how the cabinets should be placed within the kitchen. A sink cabinet can be laid out so the sink is centered beneath a window; an upper unit can be made so it won't interfere with an existing switch or light fixture. The sticks also serve as guides when building the cabinets. Lengths, widths and positions of the joints can all be marked on the material directly from the story sticks—no measurements are needed, so fewer errors are made. Story sticks make it easy to visualize construction details and are useful when assembling and installing each cabinet. In addition, if you want to alter or add to the kitchen later, the sticks provide a detailed record of the construction of the existing cabinets.

Make the sticks from wood ¼ in. to ¾ in. thick and 1½ in. wide. Light-colored woods are best because pencil marks show up better. You'll need three sticks for strip and *L*-shaped kitchens: one each for the horizontal, vertical and depth dimensions. In a Pullman kitchen, which has cabinets on opposite walls, you'll need four sticks: two horizontals (one for each wall), a vertical stick and a depth stick. A *U*-shaped kitchen requires three horizontals and a vertical—the horizontal sticks show the depths of the units on adjacent walls, as shown in the drawing at right. Mark the kitchen's upper units on one side of each stick, the lowers on the other side. Use a different-colored pencil for uppers, to identify them quickly.

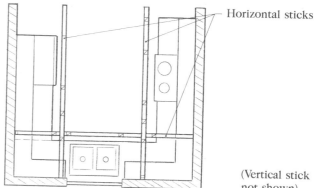

Horizontal sticks

(Vertical stick not shown)

Where cabinets are on opposite walls, such as in a *U*-shaped kitchen, you'll need four story sticks.

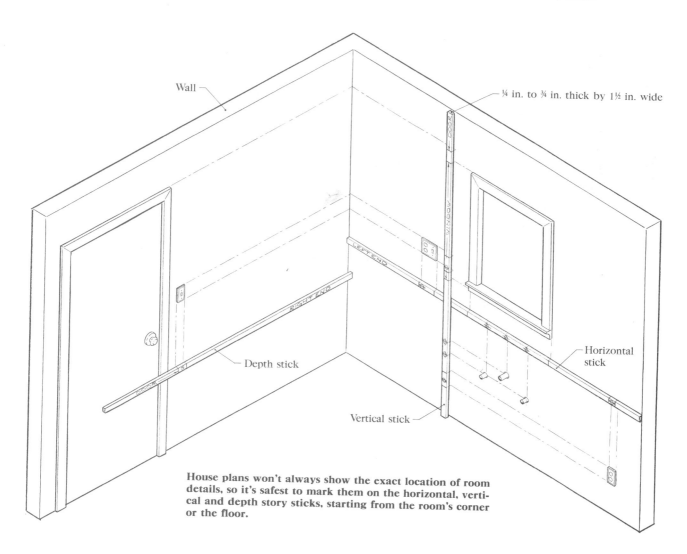

Wall

¼ in. to ¾ in. thick by 1½ in. wide

Depth stick

Horizontal stick

Vertical stick

House plans won't always show the exact location of room details, so it's safest to mark them on the horizontal, vertical and depth story sticks, starting from the room's corner or the floor.

Before the Stick Layout

Consider the following details before beginning a stick layout.

How will the cabinets be broken into units? Obviously, a complete set of cabinets can't be constructed in the shop as one unit, transported to the kitchen and installed. A good place to break is at a corner or at a tall, deep unit, like a pantry or broom closet. (Cabinet breakdown is discussed on pp. 9-11.)

Will the cabinets have a face frame or not? A face frame hides the raw edge of the plywood case parts and can be scribed to fit the contours of an irregular wall. Cabinets without face frames are sleeker looking, but you'll have to live with the rough plywood edge, or band it with thin strips of wood. (Face frames are discussed in Chapter 8.)

You must also decide how the drawers will slide, and what style drawer and door faces you want to use. Drawers can be supported and guided many ways, but I usually run them on side-hung metal slides or on wooden center guides, fastened to a shelf called a dust panel. Door and drawer faces can lie flush with the face frame (flush face), protrude half the thickness of the face beyond the face frame (lip face), or protrude the full thickness of the face (overlay face). (Door and drawer faces are discussed in Chapter 9.) Select all hardware before laying out the sticks—it's frustrating to get a cabinet built, then find you can't get the hinges you need. (Hardware is discussed in Chapter 11.)

Remember that most cabinet parts are ¾ in. thick. The exceptions are the cabinet back and drawer bottoms (¼ in.), dust panels, drawer sides and drawer backs (all ½ in.). Dadoes and rabbets are ¼ in. deep, except the rabbet at the back edge of a finish end, which is cut ½ in. by ½ in. Dadoes and rabbets are cut only in the vertical members. (Joinery is discussed in Chapter 5.)

Make sure you know the actual sizes of the major appliances to be used. Appendix 1 lists the sizes of most major appliances, but the only safe way to design around them is by referring to the manufacturer's specification sheet for each one.

Laying Out the Sticks

The importance of accuracy in stick layout cannot be overestimated. Think of the story stick as a ruler having only the marks you need. If the marks are inaccurate, problems will plague you all along the way, from cutting out the parts to installing the cabinet.

A sharp pencil is a must when laying out the sticks. It will help you make accurate marks, and if you don't, the line will be easy to erase.

Start layout with the architectural details of the kitchen, as shown in the drawing on p. 13. It's safer to rely on the sticks than on the house plans for this information, because actual construction may differ from what's on the plans. Begin layout of the vertical stick at the floor. For the horizontal and depth sticks, begin at the end or corner of the walls. Label each stick as a horizontal, vertical or depth stick.

Marking the cabinets on the story sticks is the part of layout that most people find difficult to grasp at first. Here are a couple of general rules to help you get started.

Cabinet parts should be identified by name or symbol, as shown in the drawing below. When marking out the parts, hook the tape measure on the floor

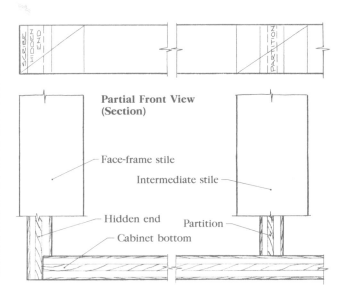

Partial Front View (Section)

Face-frame stile

Intermediate stile

Hidden end   Partition

Cabinet bottom

Use a broken line as the symbol for a dado or a rabbet joint. A diagonal line indicates a face-frame part, and the two lines it connects show the width of the part.

or wall end of the stick. This way, small errors won't multiply as layout progresses from one end of the stick to the other.

It's best to go through the layout process for each stick separately. I'll use the two cabinets shown below as models. It doesn't matter which stick you do first, but the horizontal stick requires more decisions than the other two, so I'll discuss that one first.

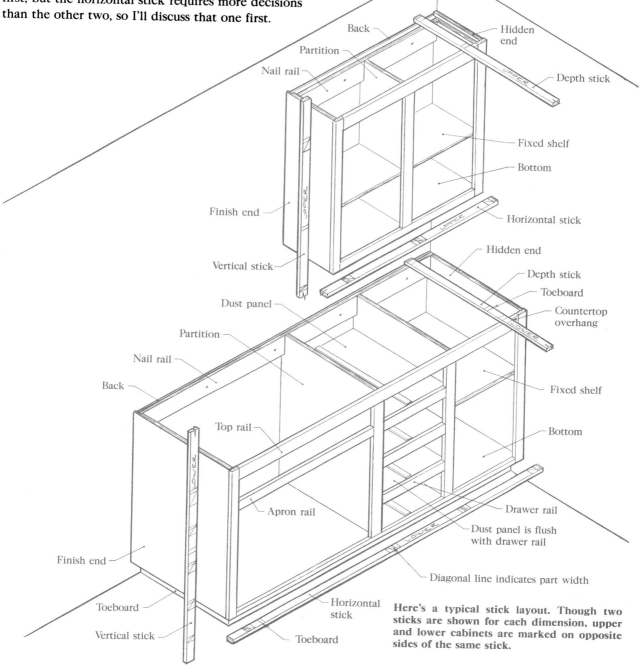

Here's a typical stick layout. Though two sticks are shown for each dimension, upper and lower cabinets are marked on opposite sides of the same stick.

The horizontal stick

1. Begin by marking the allowance for scribing at the hidden end of the cabinet. The allowance is necessary so that the face frame of the cabinet can be fit to the irregularities in the wall during installation. I generally allow about ¼ in., but if you find that the wall is really lumpy or out of plumb, allow a bit more to compensate.

3. Now mark the partitions. If you're using metal slides for the drawers, they must be mounted so they're flush with the edge of the face-frame stile. (If you can't move the partition so that it's flush with the stile's edge, you will have to fasten a filler to the partition. Try to arrange the stile and partition so that a single piece of plywood or a combination of thicknesses you have on hand can be used.)

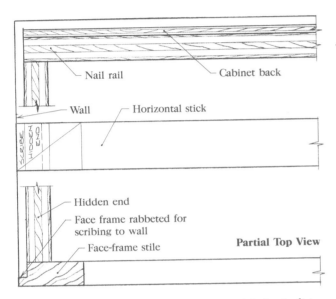

Partial Top View

The first mark on the horizontal story stick is the ¼-in. allowance for scribing at the hidden end of the cabinet. During installation, this allowance will be planed to fit the face frame to the wall.

2. Next, mark the hidden end and the depth of the dadoes or rabbets for the shelves, dust panels and the cabinet bottom.

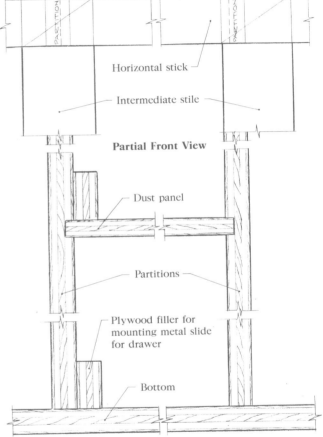

Partial Front View

Metal-slide hardware for drawers must be mounted on a partition or cabinet end, flush with the edge of the face-frame stile. If you can't make the partition flush with the stile, mount the hardware on a piece of plywood.

4. The finish end is next. The countertop usually overhangs it by 1 in., but if the end is next to a free-standing appliance, make the top flush with the end's outside face. A rabbet, cut ½ in. deep, holds the ¼-in. plywood back; mark it as a broken line. (The rabbet makes it easier to nail or staple the back in place.) A second broken line shows the depth of the dado or rabbet for the bottom, dust panel or fixed shelf.

The vertical stick

1. Start the layout of the vertical stick at the floor. Begin by marking the 4-in.-high toe space on the stick, and then mark the thickness of the cabinet bottom. If you will be using a bottom rail more than ¾ in. wide, however, you will have to make the toe-board wider to provide adequate toe space, as shown in the drawing below.

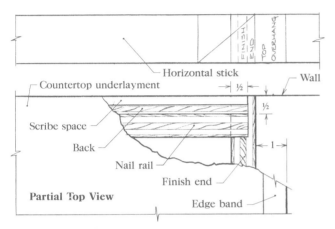

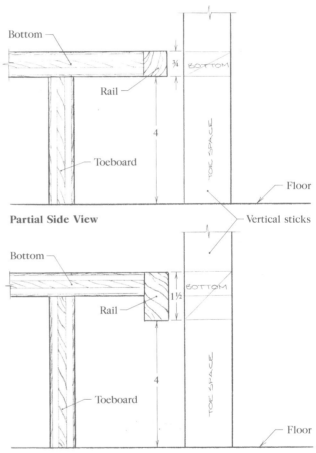

Cut a ½-in. by ½-in. rabbet on the back edge of the finish end; the resulting ¼-in. allowance for scribing allows a close fit to an irregular wall.

Lay out the toe space, then the bottom, on the vertical stick. The toe space must be 4 in.; if the bottom rail is wider than the bottom of the cabinet, you'll have to make the toeboard wider, too.

5. I usually mark the face-frame stiles last. Their width depends on the style of cabinet you choose. I discuss this in detail in Chapter 8, but in general, the stiles for flush-face cabinets are between 1¼ in. and 1½ in. wide. Lip and overlay faces will hide part of the stile, so if you want the same amount of stile to show at the end as over a partition, make the stiles over the partitions wider to compensate. Lip-face and overlay-face doors require a stile at least 2 in. wide if two doors hinge on the same stile, so that the stile can accommodate both hinges. The 60° back-bevel hinge used on overlay-face doors (p. 83) requires that intermediate stiles be at least 2½ in. wide.

2. Mark the counter. A kitchen cabinet will have an overall height of 36 in.; a bathroom vanity, 32 in.

3. Below the counter is the top rail of the face frame, usually 2½ in. wide. It's wider than the stiles because the countertop underlayment is often banded with a strip of wood about 1¼ in. wide, which covers part of the top rail. If a breadboard is to fit in the rail, the rail should be at least 2½ in. wide and extend a minimum of 1¾ in. below the band.

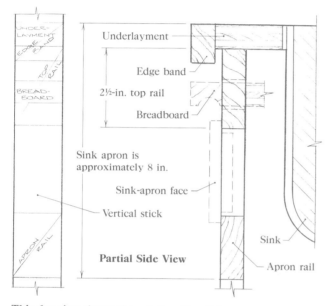

This drawing shows the relationship of the countertop, top rail, breadboard and sink apron.

4. In sink and countertop-range cabinets, an apron hides the sink or range workings from view when the doors are open. The apron and counter should measure about 8 in. wide. Incorporate the apron rail into the face frame; fill the space between it and the top rail with a false drawer face. The drawer rails should be the same width as the apron rails.

5. Consider drawer sizes next. The top face is usually the same height as the false face in the sink apron. Our sense of proportion requires that each face in a stack be the same height or slightly higher than the face above, and that rails between drawers be the same width or narrower than the stiles. A ¾-in. to 1¼-

in. drawer rail works well for lip faces; a 2-in. rail is best for overlay faces. The top edge of the rail and the top surface of the dust panel should be flush.

6. Now locate the fixed shelf, if you have one. Place it slightly above the center of the door opening, so that taller items can be placed in the bottom of the cabinet. An upper cabinet that has fixed shelves usually has two of them; the top space is greatest, so more things will be within easy reach. (Avoid shelf spans longer than 32 in., and don't mark adjustable shelving on the stick.)

If the cabinet has different shelf and drawer layouts at each end, divide the stick in half along its length and mark an end on each half.

7. Mark out the upper cabinets. A 16-in. clearance between upper and lower cabinets used to be standard, but with the increased use of portable countertop appliances, an 18-in. clearance is better.

8. In upper units, I dado the bottoms into the sides, because a dado is stronger than a rabbet. The dado is cut ½ in. to ¾ in. above the ends of the sides, and a bottom rail wider than ¾ in. is used. If no bottom rail is used, the door will overhang the bottom and you won't need a door pull. I dado the top of an upper cabinet as well, so the face frame and finish end can be scribed to the ceiling. (If the top is lowered the same amount that the bottom is raised, you'll save a machine setup when cutting the joints.)

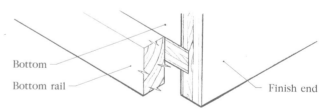

The bottoms of upper cabinets should be dadoed into the ends. (The bottoms of lowers are sometimes dadoed, too.)

9. For good looks, the top rail of the upper cabinet is usually the widest member of the face frame—3 in. to 4 in. is quite common.

10. The cabinet back is housed in a rabbet in the finish end and is butt-jointed over the back edge of

the cabinet top and hidden end. On lower cabinets, the back should be flush with the nail rail so it will be out of the way when scribing the counter. The joint between the back and the bottom of an upper cabinet may be made in two different ways, depending on the unit's height. If the bottom of the cabinet is above eye level, you'll want to fit the bottom to the wall to hide the gap between the wall and the back. Do this by making the bottom the same width as the finish end, and then setting the back in a deep rabbet. Mark the rabbet on the vertical and depth sticks. If the bottom of the cabinet is below eye level, fasten the back to the bottom with a butt joint; mark the butt joint on the depth stick. Don't let the back hang lower than the underside of the bottom because this makes squaring the cabinet during assembly difficult. (This rule applies for lower cabinets, too.)

The depth stick

1. Start the depth stick at the wall. Use both sides of the stick (one for upper cabinets, one for lower), or show both uppers and lowers on one side.

2. The overall depth of an upper cabinet should be 12¼ in. When you subtract the allowance for scribing and the thickness of the back and face frame, an 11-in.-wide shelf will remain—wide enough for the largest dinner plate. Building the upper cabinet deeper would bring it too near the front edge of the countertop, making it difficult to work at the counter.

3. The overall depth of a lower cabinet, not including the counter, is 24 in. (The countertop usually overhangs the case 1 in.) A built-in broom closet or pantry is usually made slightly deeper than the lower cabinets it fits into because joining cabinets together in the same plane is difficult to do. Mark the parts and joints for the upper and lower cabinets on the depth stick as shown in the drawing below.

A bathroom vanity is sometimes made shallower because of the smaller sink and room size. At times, these units may be as shallow as 20 in. Be sure to check on the sink size to be certain the sink will fit the cabinet.

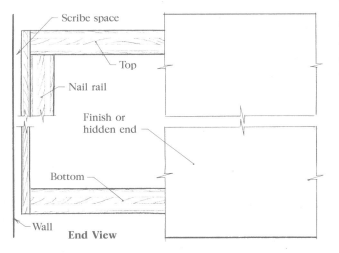

If a cabinet is below eye level, use a butt joint to fasten the bottom and back.

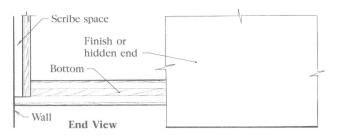

If the bottom is above eye level, join the back to it with a deep rabbet, so you can scribe the bottom to fit the wall.

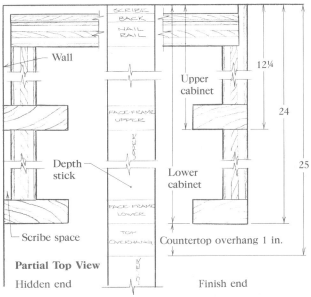

Start laying out the depth stick at the wall; mark upper and lower units on one side of the stick, or on both.

Selecting and Estimating Materials

Chapter 3

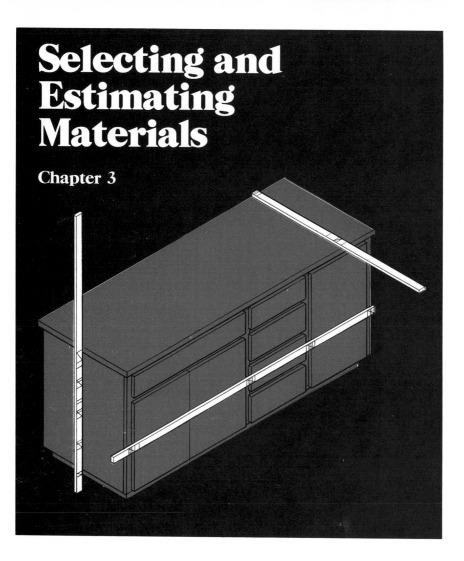

Materials, of course, are at the heart of cabinet-making. But picking a species of wood, deciding between types of plywood and solid wood, and then figuring out how much wood you'll need can be a confusing exercise. There are many books that discuss the characteristics of wood in depth, so in this chapter I'll explain the forms in which wood is available, and how to prepare an estimate of materials and a cutting list.

Lumber can be defined simply as boards cut from the tree. All lumber shrinks and swells to some extent in reaction to changes in humidity; the amount of shrinkage is greatest across the grain and least parallel to it. Because cabinets require many wide pieces (ends, bottom, back, underlayment), and wide pieces of solid wood shrink a lot, many cabinetmakers use plywood instead. Lumber is commonly used, however, for narrow pieces such as face-frame parts, edge banding and moldings.

Plywood is made from an odd number of sheets of solid wood ⅛₅ in. to ¼ in. thick (called plies). Arranging the plies so that the grain of each runs at right angles to those adjacent to it makes plywood dimensionally stable, that is, it won't shrink or swell much with changes in humidity. Plywood is available in a variety of standard thicknesses and surface dimensions. Plywood's greatest drawback is the raw look of the plies that show on the edges of the panel. There are several ways to cover these edges, however, and some are discussed in Chapter 4.

Plywood is divided into two groups, one for hardwood and one for softwood, and each is graded by a different system. The American Plywood Association administers the standards for manufacturing and grading softwood construction and industrial plywood; a summary of their grading standards is shown in the chart at right. The Hardwood Plywood Manufacturers Association provides the same information for hardwood plywoods and a few softwood plywoods, such as redwood and knotty pine.

The face veneers (the outermost plies) of construction and industrial softwood panels are graded from *A* through *D* in descending order of quality. (You can't usually find grade *N* at the local lumberyard, but a large millwork company may be able to order it for you.) You can buy a plywood panel having faces of the same grade (such as *A-A*) or of different grades (*A-C* or *B-D*); any face graded *B* or better has been sanded. For cabinet work, where both faces of the panel will show, both should be graded *B* or better.

Two other types of softwood panels—shop-grade panels and blows—are available, but are not considered true grades. Shop-grade panels have defects: something happened to them in the mill to prevent them from meeting the specifications of their intended grade. For example, a shop-grade panel may be out of square or have face veneers that are sanded through. These panels usually have one good face, and are cheaper than other grades, so I frequently use them for underlayment and hidden ends.

Blows are panels made of improperly dried plies. To cure the glue between the plies, the panels are subjected to heat and pressure. When the plies contain too much moisture, the resulting steam can cause the panels to explode (which is how blows got their name). More often, the steam inhibits the curing of the glue and causes delamination at the glue line. This delamination may appear to be confined to a small area, but when the panel is cut, the delamination often spreads. No matter how inexpensive, blows are not acceptable for cabinet parts.

A specialty grade of softwood plywood that is sometimes used in cabinetmaking is Medium Density Overlay (MDO). This plywood is covered on one or both faces with a thin, smooth, opaque, resin-fiber overlay. If you are going to paint the cabinets, MDO makes an ideal base.

Grades of Softwood Plywood

N Smooth-surface, natural-finish veneer. Select, all heartwood or all sapwood. Free of open defects. Allows not more than 6 repairs, wood only, per 4x8 panel, made parallel to grain and well matched for grain and color.

A Smooth, paintable. Not more than 18 neatly made repairs (boat, sled, or router type) parallel to grain permitted. May be used for natural finish in less demanding applications.

B Solid surface. Shims, circular repair plugs and tight knots to 1 in. across grain permitted. Some minor splits permitted.

C - Plugged. Improved C veneer with splits limited to ⅛ in. wide, and knotholes and borer holes limited to ¼ in. by ½ in. Admits some broken grain. Synthetic repairs permitted.

C Tight knots to 1½ in. Knotholes to 1 in. across grain and some to 1½ in. if total width of knots and knotholes is within specified limits. Synthetic or wood repairs. Discoloration and sanding defects that do not impair strength permitted. Limited splits allowed. Stitching permitted.

D Knots and knotholes to 2½ in. wide across grain and ½ in. larger within specified limits. Limited splits allowed. Stitching permitted. Limited to Interior, Exposure 1 and Exposure 2 panels.

The Hardwood Plywood Manufacturers Associ-ation has a different grading system. Both faces are graded, but grade symbols and criteria are not the same as for softwood plywoods. (A summary of the standards from the U.S. Department of Commerce Publication PS 51-71 is shown below.)

A hardwood-plywood panel for a cabinet should have one face graded *A* and the other graded *2* or

better. Shop-grade panels of hardwood plywood may be okay to use in cabinets of lower quality. You can cut defects from wood with nondescript grain with-out affecting appearance, but in wood with distinc-tive grain, it's difficult to trim out the defect and still match the grain in door and drawer faces.

Two other sheet materials are often used for door and drawer faces and finish ends. Particleboard is a combination of wood chips, shavings, fibers and ad-hesives bonded together under heat and pressure. It is dimensionally stable, but won't hold nails or screws as well as plywood. When it is faced with hardwood veneer or plastic laminate, particleboard is usable for face parts. (But care must be taken where particleboard faced with plastic laminate joins other parts because it cannot be sanded or planed flush.) Unfaced, it may be used for interior cabinet parts.

The other substitute for hardwood plywood is lumber-core plywood, which has a core of narrow pieces of edge-glued lumber faced with two layers of veneer on each side. Lumber-core plywood holds screws and nails well, the edges don't show as many glue lines as plywood, and the faces can be sanded. It's not as strong as hardwood plywood but is ade-quate for most cabinet construction. A big disadvan-tage is that lumber core is more expensive than com-parable thicknesses of plywood or particleboard.

So what type of material should you choose for each part of the cabinet? Here are some guidelines to help you decide.

For the interior parts, use shop-grade or *B-B* softwood plywood. I usually use *B-B* grade on smaller jobs and shop grade on larger ones, where there is more opportunity to trim or hide the defects. Parti-cleboard is acceptable, but be aware of the potential problems with nailing and screwing into the edges.

For the visible parts of the cabinet, use the best grade of hardwood plywood you can afford. Shop grade can be used for lower-quality jobs, especially when grain patterns are not a factor. Veneered parti-cleboard is okay, too, but be aware of the difficulty with nailing and screwing. If you don't object to the price, lumber core is nice to work with.

For the face frame, use ¾-in. lumber of the same species as the face veneer. Solid red alder can some-times be substituted for solid birch. (In the Pacific Northwest, red alder is a lot easier to find).

Grades of Hardwood Plywood

SP **Specialty grade.** This plywood is made to or-der to meet the specific requirements of a par-ticular buyer. The grain of the face veneers is usually specially matched.

A **Premium grade.** The face veneers are smooth and the edges tightly matched in a book-matched or slip-matched pattern.

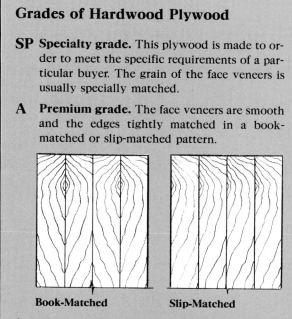

Book-Matched   **Slip-Matched**

1 **Good grade.** The face veneers are smooth and tight. If more than one piece of veneer is used on the face, the grain may not be matched, but it will not contrast sharply.

2 **Sound grade.** The face veneers are free from open defects, but discoloration and sound knots to ¾ in. in diameter and patches are per-mitted. The veneer on the face is not matched for color or grain.

3 **Utility grade.** This plywood may have tight knots to 1 in. in diameter, discoloration and slight splits. Decay is not permitted.

4 **Backing grade.** Open knotholes to 3 in. in di-ameter, open splits and joints are permitted. Grain and color are not matched.

Lists of Materials

The cabinetmaker usually makes two different lists of materials. The first is an estimate of materials, in full-sheet or board form, which may be used to bid on a job or to order the material from a supplier. The second is a cutting list: a list of cabinet parts and their exact sizes, taken from the story sticks. Samples of both these lists are shown on pp. 25-27, and blank forms are provided in Appendix 4.

As you prepare the estimate of materials, you should keep the following facts in mind.

The width of a board or a piece of plywood is always measured across the grain, and the length is measured parallel to the direction of the grain.

The most common sheet size of plywood, veneered particleboard or lumber-core plywood is 48 in. wide by 96 in. long. Special sizes can be ordered in large quantities, but these sheets are expensive.

Because you'll be cutting a number of parts from each sheet, you'll want to minimize waste and effort, while ensuring maximum strength in each part. Cabinets should be designed taking account of the size of a sheet of plywood and the most economical ways to cut it. A standard panel can be ripped along its length into two pieces slightly less than 24 in. wide, or three pieces slightly less than 16 in. wide, or four pieces slightly less than 12 in. wide. Likewise, the panel can be crosscut into pieces slightly less than 48 in., 32 in. or 24 in. long. I call these varied dimensions multiple-cut dimensions.

Plywood is strong in any direction, but it's stiffer along the face grain than across it. This is especially noticeable in thin sheets. For maximum stiffness, the grain on all the horizontal pieces of a cabinet (shelves, underlayment and bottom) should run along the length of the cabinet. The grain in the vertical pieces (ends and partitions) should run vertically. Exceptions to this rule are the cabinet back, toeboard and drawer fronts. Cut the cabinet back to make the best use of the material, regardless of grain direction. A toeboard may have the grain running either way, too, but all the toeboards in a kitchen should run the same way. In plywood drawers, horizontal grain is preferable in the sides, but vertical grain is okay—just be consistent. Drawer backs may have grain running in the direction that makes the best use of the materials. The grain in drawer bottoms can go either way, but try to run it parallel to the longest direction. The grain in drawer fronts should run vertically.

Preparing the estimate of materials—To illustrate how to prepare an estimate, I'll use the cabinet below.

1. First, list the parts. Imagine arrows being shot through the cabinet from left to right. Name each part they would hit as they pass through—in this case, a left end (finish), a partition, a left and right drawer side (they'll be cut into eight parts later), a partition, a right end (hidden), and the ends and stretchers of the toeboard.

2. Shoot down through the top in each section of the cabinet. Name common parts once. You'll list an underlayment, a shelf, three dust panels, four drawer bottoms and a bottom.

3. Shoot from the front to the back in each section, naming common parts once. Think of the door and drawer faces as one large piece. You'll list a face, face-frame parts, a drawer back (later cut into four backs), a cabinet back, the front and back of the toeboard and banding for the underlayment and shelves.

4. Look at the sketch of the cabinet and its overall dimensions and fill in estimated widths and lengths of each part on the list. Use the smallest multiple-cut dimension. If you're unsure, use the next-largest multiple-cut dimension—it's better to overestimate than underestimate. A completed estimate of materials for this cabinet is shown on the opposite page.

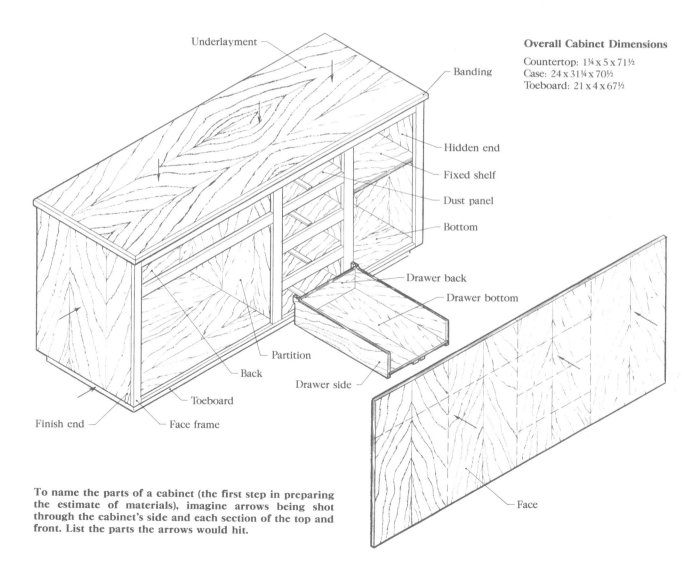

Overall Cabinet Dimensions

Countertop: 1¼ x 5 x 71½
Case: 24 x 31¼ x 70½
Toeboard: 21 x 4 x 67½

To name the parts of a cabinet (the first step in preparing the estimate of materials), imagine arrows being shot through the cabinet's side and each section of the top and front. List the parts the arrows would hit.

Estimate of Materials   **Name of Unit** SINK (OVERLAY FACE, 5/8-IN. OVERLAP ALL AROUND)

Group	No. of Parts	Name of Part	Thick.	Width	Length	Type of Material	Special Notes
PLYWOOD CASE AND DRAWER PARTS	1	LEFT END (FINISH)	3/4	24	32	HARDWOOD PLY	
	2	PARTITIONS	3/4	24	32	SOFTWOOD PLY	
	2	PANELS FOR DRAWER SIDES	1/2	32	24	SWP	
	1	RIGHT END (HIDDEN)	3/4	24	32	SWP	
	1	UNDERLAYMENT	3/4	25	72	SWP	DIMENSIONS INCLUDE BAND
	1	SHELF	3/4	24	24	SWP	
	3	DUST PANELS	1/2	24	24	SWP	ROUGH-CUT IN DOUBLE LENGTHS
	4	DRAWER BOTTOMS	1/4	16	24	SWP	
	1	BOTTOM	3/4	24	72	SWP	
	1	DRAWER AND DOOR FACE	3/4	72	32	HWP	
	1	PANEL FOR DRAWER BACKS	1/2	32 ←→ 16		SWP	GRAIN CAN RUN EITHER WAY
	1	CABINET BACK	1/4	32 ←→ 72		SWP	GRAIN CAN RUN EITHER WAY
TOEBOARD	1	TOEBOARD (FINISH END)	3/4	5	24	HWP	
	3	TOEBOARD STRETCHERS AND HIDDEN END	3/4	5	24	SWP	
	1	TOEBOARD (FRONT)	3/4	5	72	HWP	
	1	TOEBOARD (BACK)	3/4	5	72	SWP	
FACE FRAME	1	TOP RAIL	3/4	2 1/2	72	HARDWOOD	EXACT WIDTH
	3	INTERMEDIATE RAILS	3/4	2	36	HARDWOOD	MAKES 1 APRON AND 4 DRAWER RAILS
	1	BOTTOM RAIL	3/4	3/4	72	HARDWOOD	EXACT WIDTH
	1	STILE (HIDDEN END)	3/4	2	33	HARDWOOD	EXACT WIDTH
	1	STILE (FINISH END)	3/4	1 3/4	33	HARDWOOD	EXACT WIDTH
	2	INTERMEDIATE STILES	3/4	2 1/4	33	HARDWOOD	EXACT WIDTH
BANDING	1	UNDERLAYMENT EDGE BAND	3/4	1 1/4	72	PINE	EXACT WIDTH
	1	UNDERLAYMENT EDGE BAND	3/4	1 1/4	25	PINE	EXACT WIDTH
	1	SHELF EDGE BAND	3/4	1/2	24	PINE	EXACT WIDTH
MISC.	3 SETS	HINGES					
	7	PULLS					
	1	PLASTIC LAMINATE		32	96		INCLUDES TOP, BAND AND BACKSPLASH

5. To determine how many sheets of plywood you'll need, draw a rectangle representing a sheet of plywood of each thickness. (For a sample form for panel layout, see Appendix 4.) Quickly lay out on these rectangles each part from the estimate of materials. (Remember that width is measured across the grain and length parallel to the grain.)

6. To figure how much lumber you'll need for the face frame, consider the length of the cabinet; one piece at least that long is needed for the top and bottom rails. Add at least 1 in. in width to each piece for straightening, jointing and sawing. (If the top rail is to be 2½ in. wide, the bottom rail ¾ in. wide and the intermediate rails 2 in. wide, you'll need a board that is about 8 in. wide—the sum of the pieces plus 3 in. of waste—and as long as the cabinet.) The stiles are figured in the same way.

Preparing the cutting list—I find that students have difficulty keeping track of a large number of parts, so I have them make a cutting list and cut the parts for one phase of cabinet construction at a time. I work this way myself, too. After completing one phase, I make the cutting list for the next one. (If you are going to make more than one cabinet, work them all through the same phase at one time.)

The first phase of cabinet construction is cutting and assembling the basic case: ends, partitions, fixed shelves, dust panels, bottom and back. The second phase is assembling the face frame, and gluing and nailing it to the case. (Some cabinetmakers prefer to make the face frame before the case. The frame helps them visualize the cabinet, and they can take it to the site to check its fit. The frame is fragile, though, so there is risk of damaging it if you're not careful.) The third phase is building the doors and drawers; and the fourth phase is making toeboards and underlayments for the lower units.

Name each part on the cutting list in the same way as on the estimate of materials. Then take the measurements of each part directly from the story sticks, as shown in the drawing on p. 20. It's hard to get accurate measurements if you measure from the hooked end of a steel tape, so I measure from the tape's 10-in. mark. Just remember to subtract 10 in. from the reading. The chart below shows the cutting list for the sink cabinet shown in the drawing on p. 24.

Cutting List   Name of Unit SINK (OVERLAY FACE, 5/8-IN. OVERLAP ALL AROUND)

	No. of Parts	Name of Part	Thick.	Width R F	Length R F	Type of Material	Special Notes
	1	LEFT END (FINISH)	¾	23½	31¼	HWP	DADO SHELF, RABBET BOTTOM
	2	PARTITIONS	¾	23	30½	SWP	DADO SHELF AND DUST PANELS
	1	RIGHT END (HIDDEN)	¾	23	31¼	SWP	INCLUDES ¼-IN. SCRIBE ALLOWANCE
	1	FIXED SHELF	¾	23	17¼	SWP	INCLUDES BANDING
	3	DUST PANELS	½	23	17	SWP	ROUGH-CUT AS UNIT
	1	BOTTOM	¾	23	69¼	SWP	
	1	BACK	¼	31¼	70	SWP	GRAIN CAN RUN EITHER WAY

	No. of Parts	Name of Part	Thick.	Width	R	F	Length	R	F	Type of Material	Special Notes
FACE FRAME	1	TOP RAIL	3/4	2 1/2			72			HARDWOOD	
	1	APRON RAIL	3/4	2			36			HARDWOOD	ALL LENGTHS
	3	DRAWER RAILS	3/4	2			16			HARDWOOD	APPROXIMATE.
	1	BOTTOM RAIL	3/4	3/4			72			HARDWOOD	USE STOP-BLOCK
	1	STILE (HIDDEN END)	3/4	2			33			HARDWOOD	SYSTEM TO CUT
	1	STILE (FINISH END)	3/4	1 3/4			33			HARDWOOD	EXACT LENGTH
	2	INTERMEDIATE STILES	3/4	2 1/4			33			HARDWOOD	
DOOR/DRAWER FACES	1	RIGHT DOOR	3/4	16 1/4			29 1/4			HWP	
	1	DRAWER FACE	3/4	16 1/4			5 3/4			HWP	CUT DRAWER FACES
	3	DRAWER FACES	3/4	16 1/4			7			HWP	FROM ONE PANEL
	1	SINK-APRON FACE	3/4	33 1/2			5 3/4			HWP	
	1	DOOR PANEL	3/4	33 1/2			22 3/4			HWP	SPLIT INTO TWO
DRAWER PARTS (EXCEPT FACE)	2	DRAWER SIDES	1/2	4 1/2			23 1/16			SWP	LENGTH IS LESS 3/4-IN. TO ALLOW FOR NAIL RAIL
	6	DRAWER SIDES	1/2	5 3/4			23 13/16			SWP	
	1	FALSE FRONT	1/2	4 1/2			14 1/4			SWP	
	3	FALSE FRONTS	1/2	5 3/4			14 1/4			SWP	
	4	DRAWER BOTTOMS	1/4	14 1/4			23 1/16			SWP	
	1	DRAWER BACK	1/2	3 5/8			14 1/4			SWP	
	3	DRAWER BACKS	1/2	4 7/8			14 1/4			SWP	
TOEBOARD	1	TOEBOARD (FRONT)	3/4	4			67 1/2			HWP	INCLUDES 1/4-IN.
	1	TOEBOARD (FINISH END)	3/4	4			21 1/4			HWP	SCRIBE ALLOWANCE
	1	TOEBOARD (BACK)	3/4	4			66 3/4			SWP	
	3	TOEBOARD STRETCHERS	3/4	4			19			SWP	
UNDERLAYMENT	1	TOP UNDERLAYMENT	3/4	24 1/2			70 3/4			SWP	INCLUDES 1/4-IN.
	1	TOP EDGE BAND	3/4	1 1/4			71 1/2			PINE	SCRIBE ALLOWANCE
	1	TOP EDGE BAND	3/4	1 1/4			24 1/2			PINE	

Preparing the Materials

Chapter 4

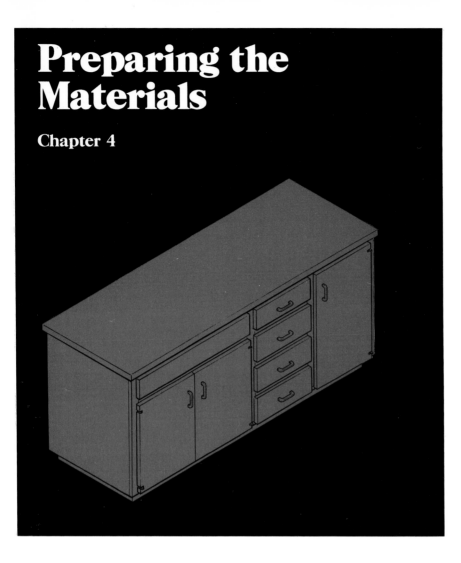

When you've completed the story sticks, bought the material and made the cutting list for the case, you're ready to cut the parts out roughly to size. This might appear to be unnecessary, but I find rough-cutting makes it possible to produce the finish cuts with much more accuracy. There are two reasons for this. First, a sheet of ¾-in. plywood weighs about 75 lb. and can be awkward to handle and feed through the tablesaw. Second, it often takes longer to set up the saw for an accurate cut than it does to make the cut. By rough-cutting first, and making all finish cuts of the same dimension at the same time, you'll cut down on the number of setups you'll need.

How oversized should the rough cuts be? There should be enough extra material so that there will be wood on the waste side of the sawblade during the finish cut. (If the blade encounters resistance on one side only, it will tend to wander away from the work.) Generally, cut ¾ in. to 1 in. extra in width and in length. The extra length should be the same on all the parts, if possible, to avoid confusion later. For rough-cutting, use a blade that makes a wide kerf; it's easy to twist the pieces of plywood when sawing, and a blade without good clearance will bind. I prefer a 10-in. carbide blade with 60 to 72 teeth, ground for both crosscutting and ripping, but a 10-in. ripping blade will work, too. When you are rough-cutting on the tablesaw, always work with the good face of the plywood up. The blade may chip out the bottom face as it exits the cut, particularly when crosscutting.

Rough-Cutting

1. Most cases have at least one finish end. Chalk it out on the hardwood plywood, along with the blanks for the door and drawer faces (p. 60). (Don't lean on the chalk too heavily because the marks can be hard to remove later.) Transfer the dimensions from the story sticks, allowing for extra length and width. I take my time doing this, so I can figure out the best way to use the grain. When making several cabinets, I lay out all the parts to be cut from the hardwood plywood at once, to take advantage of the grain patterns and avoid waste.

2. If there are any unused strips wider than 4 in., they can be used for toeboards. Rip them off before cutting out the finish end for the case.

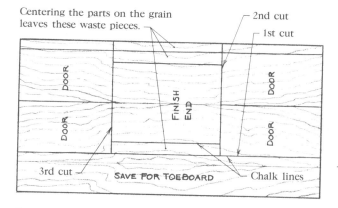

Centering the parts on the grain leaves these waste pieces.

2nd cut
1st cut
DOOR
DOOR
FINISH END
DOOR
DOOR
3rd cut
SAVE FOR TOEBOARD
Chalk lines

Lay out the hardwood-plywood panels carefully. Even though you won't be cutting out door and drawer faces at this stage, it's worth taking the time to arrange the parts so that each cabinet will have similar grain patterns.

A plywood sheet can be hard to handle, so when ripping, have an assistant help start the cut, then move to suppport the sheet as it comes off the saw. If you don't have an assistant, you can build a roller support (p. 109). After completing the cut, turn off the saw before maneuvering the pieces off the table.

3. Crosscut the blanks for the door and drawer faces and finish ends to rough length (usually 32 in.). Rip the finish end from one 32-in. blank, and set aside the remainder of the hardwood plywood.

4. Now rip the softwood plywood for the rest of the case to rough width. Use the cutting list to help make a quick layout on paper to determine how much plywood you'll need. A quick glance down the width column will reveal that the widest part will be the back: 31¼ in. All the other parts will be less than 24 in. wide. Though you don't need the underlayment at this stage, you should save a piece of material for it that is at least 24½ in. wide.

The rip fence of most tablesaws can be set up to 25 in. from the blade, so all cuts along the length can be made against the fence. Wider pieces, like the cabinet back, can be cut to width by setting the fence to cut off the waste, as shown in the drawing below. This cut is about as accurate as you will get, so cut to finish width. For example, to cut a 31¼-in.-wide back from a 4-ft.-wide sheet, set the fence 16¾ in. from the far side of the blade so the kerf falls in the waste. (Your cut may be slightly crooked, so index against the factory-machined edge when cutting pieces to length and squaring the cabinet during assembly.)

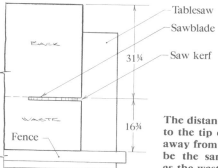

Tablesaw
Sawblade
Saw kerf
BACK
31¼
WASTE
Fence
16¾

The distance from the fence to the tip of a sawtooth set away from the fence should be the same measurement as the waste.

5. Crosscut the parts to rough length. This can be done easily and safely on a panel saw, radial arm saw (if it has the capacity), or a tablesaw equipped with a cutoff box (p. 112). (I never crosscut on the tablesaw freehand.) It's possible to rough-cut with portable power or handsaws, but I don't recommend them for finish-cutting. A note on safety: If several shelves or dust panels are shorter than they are wide, leave them ganged together or on the end of another part the same width, and rip them to finish width later.

Edge Treatment

The raw edges of plywood are ugly. You can see glue lines and, in cheaper grades, rectangular holes called core voids. So before the rough-cut plywood parts are trimmed to finish dimensions, all the edges of the case that might be seen should be covered. This includes all the case edges not hidden by the face frame, the front edges of the shelves and the bottom (if the cabinet is designed without a bottom rail).

There are several methods for covering plywood edges, but I usually use wood tape or solid-wood banding. Wood tape is a strip of wood about ½₂ in. thick and ¾ in. to 3 in. wide, usually sold in long rolls. Some wood tape is treated on one side with pressure-sensitive or heat-sensitive glue (which can be ironed onto the plywood edge). Use contact cement for tape with no glue backing. I don't have my students joint or hand-plane the edge to be banded. If a good sawblade is used to cut the plywood, it will leave a smoother edge than a novice will be able to obtain using a jointer or a plane. After applying the tape, lightly sand off the excess.

The advantage of wood tape is that it's easy to apply and so thin that the glue line is hardly noticeable. However, wood tape is not very durable, so it shouldn't be used where a lot of wear is expected—on a shelf, for example.

Solid-wood banding hides the raw edge, and also improves the screw-holding capacity of a plywood panel. This is important if you're hanging doors on a case without a face frame. Pine is usually used to band interior case parts, but the bands can match the wood used for the face frame and the face veneer of the hardwood plywood. Try not to work with bands wider than ½ in., because they're more difficult to trim flush with the face of the plywood.

To make solid-wood banding, select a piece of straight-grained lumber that is slightly thicker than the plywood and wide enough to yield the number of bands needed. (Bands the same thickness as the plywood will be difficult to get flush, but bands a little thicker can be trimmed easily.) Machine-joint (or hand-plane) the edge of the wood and rip off a band ¹⁄₁₆ in. wider than the finish width, as shown in the drawing above. The distance between the fence and the blade is narrow, so be sure to use a push stick to

finish the cut. Joint and rip as many bands as necessary. (Don't try to joint the other side of the band after ripping. It's safer to joint it after attaching it to the plywood.)

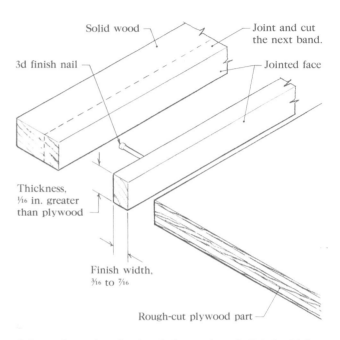

Joint and cut the edge bands from a board slightly thicker than the plywood and wide enough to make the necessary number of bands. Then glue and nail the bands to the plywood edge.

Glue and nail or glue and clamp the bands in place, putting the jointed edge against the plywood. Yellow or white glue is excellent for this job, though they both set fast and you must work quickly. Apply just enough so that a few tiny beads appear at the joint when the band is nailed or clamped in place. (If no beads appear, you risk a starved joint; more than a few beads means you're wasting glue, which creates extra work in cleanup.)

Nailing the bands in place is quicker than clamping, but there will be nail holes to fill. Three-penny (3d) finish nails 10 in. to 12 in. apart will usually be sufficient, but a check of the glue line will tell when an extra nail is needed. Keep the nails at least 1½ in. in from the ends, so the nails won't get in the way of the saw when the panel is trimmed to its finish size. At times, you may not want the nail holes to show, especially if banding the hardwood plywood. In these situations, glue and clamp, but be sure to use heavy backing boards made of scrap to ensure even pressure, or clamp two parts together to make sure the joints are tight.

When the glue has set, trim the band flush. Use a hand plane for a few pieces or an edge-band trimmer (p. 119) if you have a lot to do. An edge-band trimmer is also good to use if the wood is hard to plane.

When using a plane, rest as much of its sole on the plywood as possible. Position the corner of the plane iron along the glue line; move the plane parallel to the glue line so it won't dig into the plywood. By keeping the heel of the plane on the plywood, you'll avoid beveling the band.

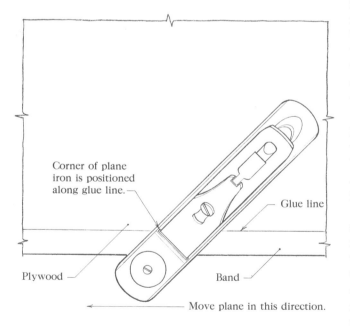

Corner of plane iron is positioned along glue line.

Glue line

Plywood

Band

Move plane in this direction.

Plane the band flush with the plywood by moving the corner of the plane iron parallel to the glue line.

Now joint the face of the edge band. Set the jointer for a ¹⁄₁₆-in. cut, or use a hand plane. If the band was nailed in place, set the nails deeper than the amount of wood to be removed.

Finish-Cutting

When the parts for the basic case have been rough-cut and edge-banded where necessary, you are ready to cut them to finish size. During finish-cutting, you will also correct any pieces that have been rough-cut out of square. The squaring process involves making the two edges parallel, then crosscutting each of the ends at 90° to the parallel edges. (The edge of a board always runs parallel to the face grain; the end runs at right angles to it.) Setting up a tablesaw, radial arm saw or panel saw for an accurate cut often takes more time than making the cut itself, so you should take full advantage of every setup by cutting all the parts of the same width or length at one time. This procedure will not only save time, but will increase accuracy, too.

I make all finish cuts on the tablesaw, ripping to finish width against the rip fence, and crosscutting to finish length with the cutoff box. Because the saw-blade tears out slightly as it exits the cut, finish-cut with the good face of the plywood up. I usually use the same carbide blade for finish-cutting as for rough-cutting, but if I find the blade tears out too much wood, I'll go to an 8-in. plywood combination blade.

1. To rip a part to width so that its edges are parallel, one edge must be straight. This edge bears against the rip fence. On parts having banded edges, use the banded edge, which has already been straightened. Joint or hand-plane a straight edge on unbanded parts, if necessary.

2. Set up the saw carefully, and remember that the saw kerf must fall in the waste. For pieces less than 25 in. wide, the finish piece should be cut between the fence and the blade: measure to the tip of a tooth that is set toward the fence, as shown in the drawing on p. 32. For pieces more than 25 in. wide, the waste must fall between the blade and fence: measure to the tip of a tooth that is set away from the fence. (This setup is also shown on p. 29.)

Many rip fences move slightly when locked down or don't lock parallel to the miter-gauge slot. Check for parallel by measuring from each end of the fence to the slot. The best check for size is to rip about ½ in. into the piece, then remove the piece from the saw and measure. Each part is approximately 1 in. overlong, so this test cut won't destroy the part.

Be sure to cut all the widest parts first, then cut the narrower ones. As each part is ripped, mark it off in the correct column on the cutting list to keep track of your progress.

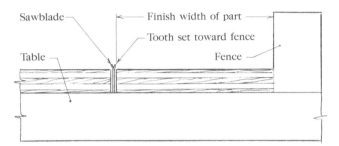

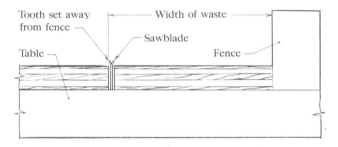

Set up the saw so that the kerf falls in the waste. Where the cabinet part is between the blade and the fence, measure to the tip of a tooth set toward the fence. Where the waste comes between, measure to the tip of a tooth set away from the fence.

3. Now crosscut all the parts to length. The miter gauges that come with most tablesaws are too small to use for crosscutting large, wide pieces. The cutoff box works much better. The push bar provides a long indexing surface, and the length between the push bar and the back bar accommodates pieces up to 48 in. wide. Two guide strips, placed at right angles to the bars, slide in the grooves milled in the tablesaw, ensuring a square cut.

You can't assume that either end of a part is square to its edges, so both ends must be trimmed. Starting with the longest part, place the banded edge away from the push bar and trim one end. Try to make the cut so that there is wood on both sides of the sawblade, and then the blade won't wander. But be sure not to cut off too much, because the other end must still be trimmed.

4. Measure and mark the pieces to finish length and, starting with the largest parts, crosscut to final length. Anytime two or more parts are the same length, you can clamp a stop block to the push bar to ensure the lengths are identical. (Remember to put the already-trimmed end against the stop.) Some pieces differ in length by a constant amount; for example, the partitions are ¾ in. shorter than the ends. Set up the stop block and cut the ends, then place a ¾-in. spacer against the stop block and cut the partitions. As each piece is cut to final length, mark it off on the cutting list.

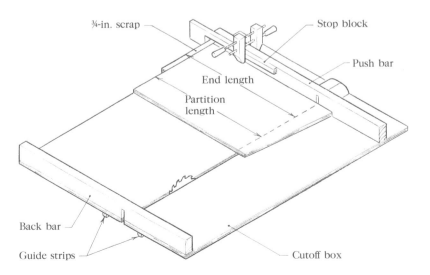

A homemade cutoff box helps in crosscutting large pieces. A stop block clamped to the push bar lets you cut parts of the same size accurately. You can cut smaller pieces without resetting the stop block by using spacers of scrap wood.

Confession Time

How many parts were cut too small? Be honest. Remember that a craftsman is not a person who doesn't make a mistake, but one who can correct or hide it.

Correcting narrow parts—If the part is too narrow, glue a solid-wood patch on one edge. (Plywood patches are too weak to use.) A patch on a finish end should match the color and grain of the plywood; usually you will want to glue the patch to the edge that will be at the back of the cabinet. Make the patch slightly thicker than the plywood to allow for a little movement as you glue it on. The patch should also be wider than you need because it's difficult to get a tight joint with a narrow patch. (If you nail the patch on rather than clamp it, don't drive the nails home—this way, you can pull them out easily later.) When the glue has cured, plane the patch flush with the face of the plywood, and then rip the part to the correct width.

Correcting short parts—Mistakes in length can also be patched, but because the grain runs at a right angle to the length of the patch, these repairs pose special problems with regard to strength and appearance. A solid-wood patch with grain running in the same direction as the plywood grain would have little strength (because of the end-grain gluing surface) and would be extremely difficult to cut and fit. It's better to use the same patches that were suggested for use on narrow parts and make them as inconspicuous as possible. A face frame will hide the end grain of most patches. (If you are not using a face frame, you may want to add a strip of banding along the front edge to cover the patch.) If the part cannot be fixed using one of the methods for patching recommended below, cut a new part and use the old one for something else.

Strength is the only consideration when patching the hidden ends of cabinets. A hidden end of an upper cabinet can take up to a ¼-in. patch at either or both ends without weakening the joint. The hidden end of a lower unit can accept a patch up to 1 in. at the top of the end. I don't like to patch the bottom of a hidden end because the patch will often break when the cabinet bottom is nailed on.

A lengthening patch on the finish end of an upper cabinet should be less than ¼ in. thick and applied to the bottom end. If you add a patch to the finish end of one upper cabinet, add the same size patch to all the finish ends—the patches will look like a deliberate way of covering the plywood edges.

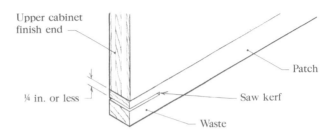

Lengthen a finish end on an upper cabinet by gluing a ¼-in. (or smaller) patch on the bottom.

On the finish end of a lower cabinet, use a ½-in.-wide patch. Put the patch on the top end so the 1¼-in. countertop banding will just hide it.

Lengthening patches on horizontal plywood parts (bottoms, dust panels, fixed shelves) should be less than ¼ in. to fall inside the dado or rabbet.

If the back of the unit is no more than ¼ in. too narrow or short, it can still be attached to the cabinet and present no problem. It must have at least one square corner and edges nearly parallel. If the back is more than ¼ in. off, it can be cut and joined to another piece over a partition or fixed shelf.

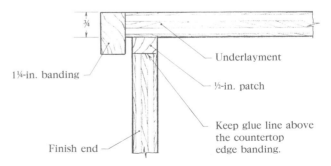

The banding on the counter will just hide a patch on the finish end of a lower cabinet.

Case Joinery

Chapter 5

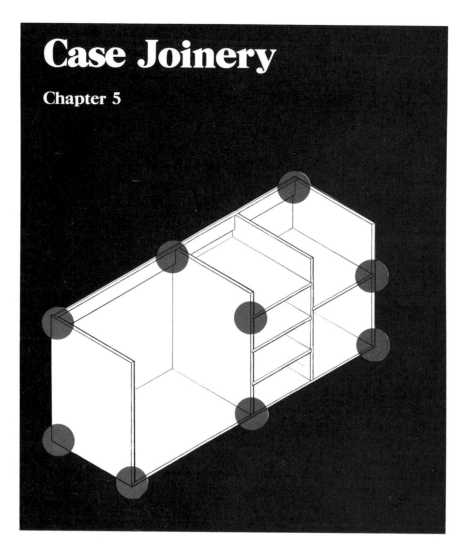

Though there are a number of woodworking joints, the kitchen cabinetmaker uses only a select few, choosing those that are easy to make and that satisfy the strength requirements of each situation. When building a basic case, I rely on rabbet, butt and dado joints to meet most of my needs. For cabinet face frames and toeboards, I use dowel joints and miter joints, respectively. Some cabinetmakers expand their repertoires to include dovetails and mortise-and-tenon joints.

The drawings above and on the opposite and following pages show the joints in typical upper and lower cases. On a lower case, the bottom is rabbeted or dadoed to the ends. (Use a rabbet if you want the bottom rail of the face frame to be ¾ in. wide; a dado if you want a wider bottom rail.) Partitions are attached to the bottom with butt joints. The finish end is rabbeted to take the back. The hidden end and partitions are notched, and the finish end rabbeted to take the nail rail. Dust panels and fixed shelves are dadoed into the partitions and ends. The countertop underlayment is usually butt-jointed and nailed to the cabinet after it is installed. All the joints are glued and nailed.

The joinery in a typical upper case is much the same as in a lower, but both the top and bottom are set into dadoes that are ¼ in. deep.

In this chapter, I'll discuss cutting the joints for the basic case. (Dowel and miter joints are explained in the chapters on the face frame and toeboard.)

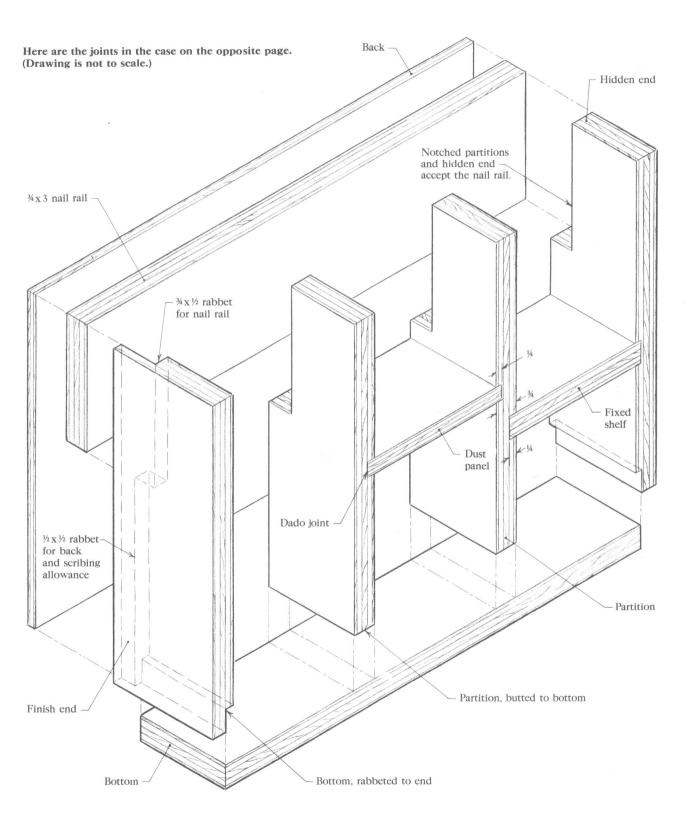

Here are the joints in the case on the opposite page.
(Drawing is not to scale.)

Back

Hidden end

Notched partitions
and hidden end
accept the nail rail.

¾ x 3 nail rail

¾ x ½ rabbet
for nail rail

¼

¾

Fixed
shelf

Dust
panel

¼

½ x ½ rabbet
for back
and scribing
allowance

Dado joint

Partition

Finish end

Partition, butted to bottom

Bottom

Bottom, rabbeted to end

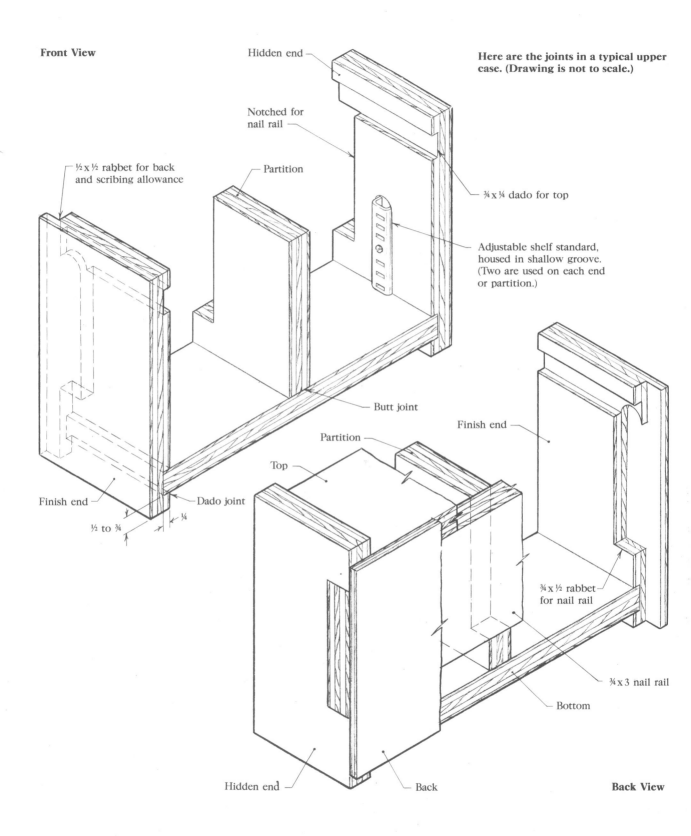

Front View

Hidden end

Here are the joints in a typical upper case. (Drawing is not to scale.)

Notched for nail rail

½ x ½ rabbet for back and scribing allowance

Partition

¾ x ¼ dado for top

Adjustable shelf standard, housed in shallow groove. (Two are used on each end or partition.)

Butt joint

Top

Partition

Finish end

Finish end

Dado joint

½ to ¾   ¼

¾ x ½ rabbet for nail rail

¾ x 3 nail rail

Bottom

Hidden end

Back

Back View

The Strength of Joints

Joints are often the weakest part of a cabinet. When structural failure occurs, it is usually at a joint, so strength should be the major concern when choosing a joint for each situation. Appearance matters too, of course, as does a joint's ability to locate itself. (The latter quality is especially important during assembly—for example, the two members of a dado joint hold themselves together, but the members of a butt joint must be held with clamps or fasteners.) The strength of a joint is affected by several factors: grain direction, wood movement in response to changing moisture content, and stress.

In glue joints, the weakest bond is between two end-grain surfaces. Edge grain to edge or face grain makes a reasonably strong glue joint. End grain glued to edge or face grain should be reinforced with dowels, screws or nails.

Variations in the moisture content of wood can cause dramatic dimensional changes in wide pieces of solid lumber. However, most of the parts of a kitchen cabinet are plywood, which is relatively stable, so it isn't necessary to be overly concerned about wood movement. The solid-wood, face-frame parts are so narrow that dimensional change is of little concern there, too.

All joints are susceptible to several different types of stress: compression, shear, tension and bending. The drawings below illustrate the forces at work and the ways in which several different joints are affected by them.

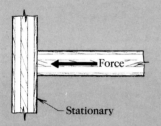

Compression stress occurs when one piece is pushed against another.

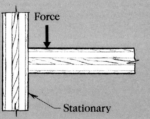

Shear stress occurs when one piece tries to move past another.

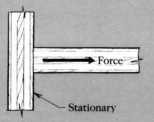

Tension occurs when one piece is pulled away from another.

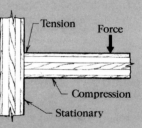

Pieces under bending stress are in both compression and tension.

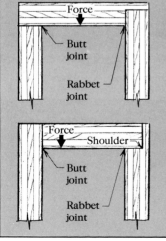

In this example, the butt joint is stronger than the rabbet. The rabbet is weakened by the removal of wood to house the vertical member, and so the joint is less likely to withstand stress.

The rabbet is stronger than the butt in this example, because the rabbet shoulder supports the horizontal member.

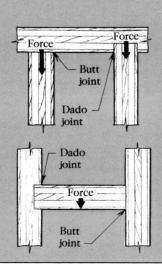

In this example, the dado is stronger because it has more gluing surface.

The dado is stronger than the butt here because, like the shoulder of the rabbet, it houses the horizontal member. The butt depends on mechanical fasteners.

Equipment for Cutting Joints

Dadoes and rabbets can be cut with a dado head on a tablesaw or radial arm saw, or with an overarm or hand router. I recommend using the hand router, but I'll discuss the merits and shortcomings of each tool.

A dado head is essentially a stack of chippers sandwiched between two sawblades—the combination of chippers and blades controls the width of the cut. On the tablesaw, a wide board can be dadoed by pushing one end along the rip fence. Because the cut is on the underside of the board, you can't gauge its progress, so blind or stopped dadoes require some guesswork. (If you're dadoing warped wood, the depth of the dado will vary with the undulations in the board, and the cabinet will be difficult to assemble.)

When dadoing on a radial arm saw, the wood is held on the table and the dado head pulled over it, so the operator can monitor the cut as it's being made. Using the radial arm saw, dadoes can be made at any angle to the edge or end of the board. However, the length of the dado is limited by the length of the radial arm, and only the larger saws can dado completely across a 24-in.-wide piece. You can cut long dadoes by turning the sawblade to cut parallel to the fence, locking it in place, and pushing the wood through against the fence—but this isn't as safe as using a tablesaw. For an accurate depth of cut, the arm must always be kept absolutely parallel to the table—a difficult adjustment to make and hold.

An overarm router (also called a pin router) is a router fixed to an arm extending over a table. Either the router or the table can be moved up and down, making this tool ideal for plunge-cutting blind dadoes. Industrial overarm routers are large and expensive; most of the smaller models that are within a home craftsman's budget lack the power and weight necessary for precise work.

A hand router between ⅞ HP and 1¼ HP, with a small set of bits, is an excellent tool for cutting dadoes and rabbets. The router allows the operator to watch the cut being made, so blind dadoes are easy. A router can be used to make a wide variety of angled dadoes, and unlike the other tools I've mentioned, it can cut dadoes of uniform depth on warped pieces with no problem. With the convex side up, the small base of the router follows the contours of a warped board to make a uniform cut. (Even when the concave side is up, the bridging effect of the small router base is so small that it needn't be of concern.) Probably the most serious disadvantage to using a router for dadoing and rabbeting is the time it takes to set up the cut.

Even though a router is inexpensive when compared with stationary power tools, a set of bits can add considerably to the bill. Most router bits are available in either high-speed steel or carbide. The initial cost of a high-speed steel bit is low, but its life between sharpenings is only a fraction of that of a carbide bit. For this reason, maintenance costs of a high-speed steel bit may soon exceed the savings.

There are other considerations you should be aware of when buying a bit—number and length of flutes, shank diameter and length. The flute is the cutting edge of the bit. The more flutes there are, the more cuts are made per minute and the smoother the cut will be. I prefer two flutes on bits larger than ¼ in. in diameter. (I think two flutes on anything smaller affects the strength.) Flute length should be determined by the maximum depth of cut—add about ¼ in. so the bit may be sharpened several times. If the flute is too long, it will cut too far from the supporting chuck of the router and vibrate.

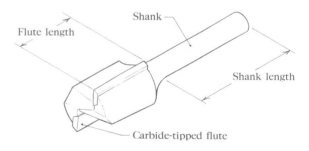

Here are the parts of a router bit.

Standard shank diameters are ½ in., ⅜ in. and ¼ in. (which is most common). Bits having large-diameter shanks are stronger and vibrate less, but most routers under 1½ HP take only ¼-in. shank bits. The shank should be as short as possible to avoid vibration, but still nearly fill the chuck.

Laying Out and Cutting the Joints

1. The first step in layout is putting the vertical parts (ends and partitions) together like pages in a book, as shown in the drawing at right. Position the parts in the book so that any defects, such as knots, won't show when the cabinet is put together. Number the top front corner of each part. Be sure not to use the same number twice, even for the parts of a second or third cabinet.

2. Now open the book to the first piece. Transfer the marks from the vertical story stick to that piece and to the mating face of the second piece. When marking out an upper case, index the story stick at the bottom of both of the ends. Any error in the lengths of these pieces will then be at the top of the case, where it can be covered by molding or scribed to the ceiling. (If the error were at the bottom, it would have to be planed off, which is hard to do neatly.) On the lower case, index the story stick against the top of the partitions and ends; if the ends are less than 1/16 in. off, the cabinet's appearance won't be affected. Mark the other face of the second piece and one face of the next piece in the same manner. Continue like this until the joints are laid out on all the pieces.

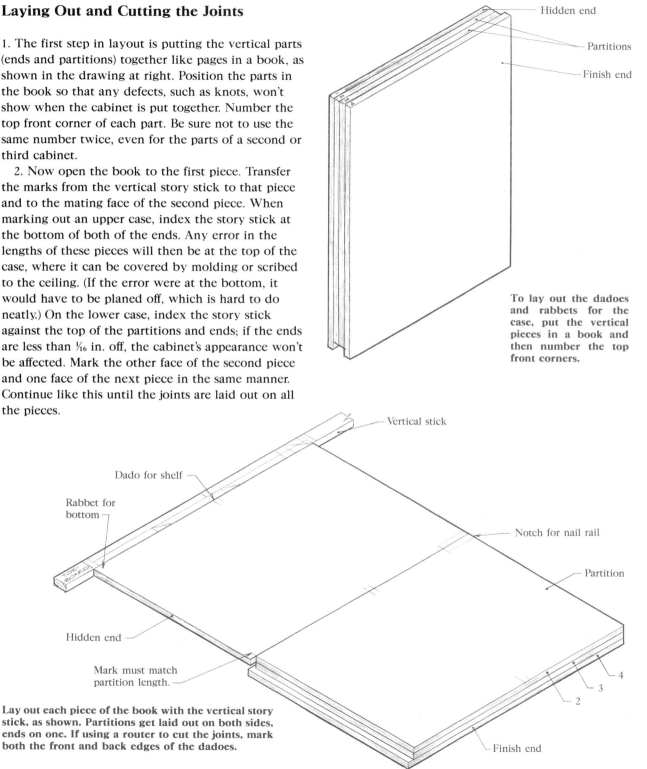

To lay out the dadoes and rabbets for the case, put the vertical pieces in a book and then number the top front corners.

Lay out each piece of the book with the vertical story stick, as shown. Partitions get laid out on both sides, ends on one. If using a router to cut the joints, mark both the front and back edges of the dadoes.

3. I'll explain how to cut the joints with a hand router, ¾-in. straight bit and straightedge fence. (The straight bits used for cutting dadoes are usually designated by their cutting diameter—a ¾-in. bit cuts a ¾-in.-wide dado.) The dadoes and rabbets for the basic case are all ¼ in. deep. A deeper dado is unnecessary, and two deep dadoes on opposite sides of a partition would seriously weaken the partition. After setting the bit to depth, make test cuts in the edge of two pieces of scrap. Putting the two test dadoes together will let you see the error doubled.

Though the plywood for the shelf and the router bit are both nominally ¾ in., they probably won't be a perfect match. Check this by fitting a shelf or dust panel into a test dado. If the dado is more than 1/64 in. too wide, drop down to the next-smallest router bit. This dado will be too narrow, but it's easy to fit the horizontal piece to a smaller dado by rabbeting the ends. (Don't try to widen the dado.)

4. The dado is cut by running the router base against a straightedge fence clamped to the partition or end. I use a bit gauge to help set the fence at the proper distance from the layout marks for the dadoes. The gauge is a piece of thin plywood or plastic, as wide as the distance from the edge of the router base to the cutting edge of the bit. (See p. 121 for how to make bit gauges.) Align one edge of the bit gauge's slot with the dado mark that's closest to the fence. Push the fence against the gauge, clamp it in position, and then remove the gauge. Set up the fence in the same manner to rout the rabbets on the hidden end and finish end.

5. Make the cut with the fence in place. Whether the cut is straight or not depends on the direction in which you push the router; the correct direction is shown in the drawing below. Rout all the ¾-in. dadoes and rabbets on each piece before moving on to the next. Work systematically: hidden end, partitions, finish end. Dadoes for dust panels are ½ in. wide, so change the bit before machining them.

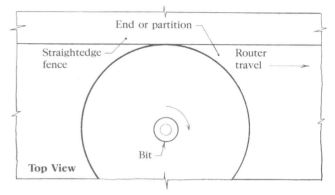

A router pushed in the direction shown will cut straight, because as the bit hits the wood, it is pushed toward the fence. If the router were pushed in the opposite direction, the bit would push away from the fence, making the router difficult to control.

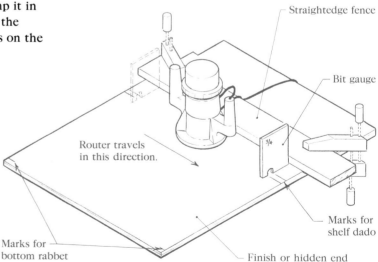

The bit gauge helps in setting up a router by making it easy to adjust the fence to the correct distance from the dado marks.

If the dadoes and rabbets will be covered by a face frame, run the router through the front edges of the plywood. If you're not using a face frame and have banded the plywood edges, make the dadoes blind—that is, stop the router approximately ½ in. from the front edge. Later on, the front edges of the shelves, dust panels and bottom will be shaped to be flush with the front edges of the ends and partitions.

6. Rout the ½-in. by ½-in. rabbet in the back edge of the finish end after all the other dadoes and rabbets are cut. You'll need a long fence and you should make the cut in two passes. Make the first pass approximately ¼ in. deep and then, without moving the fence, set the bit to ½ in. deep and make the second pass. You can also cut this rabbet on the tablesaw, as shown in the drawing below. (Be sure to use a push stick to push the waste through, or the waste could kick back at you.)

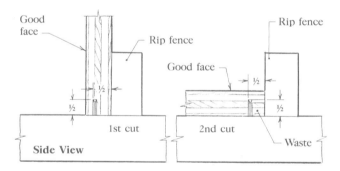

To cut the ½-in. by ½-in. rabbet in the back edge of the finish end, raise the blade ½ in. above the table, and move the fence ½ in. from the outside of the blade. Make the first cut with the piece on edge, its good face away from the fence. Use the same setup for the second cut, with the good face up on the table.

7. Now rout the short rabbet for the nail rail in the finish end. Set up the fence with the bit gauge as before. On an upper case, rout out just the width of the rail and square off the cut with a chisel. A nail rail in a lower case won't show, so it won't matter if the rabbet is longer and not squared off.

8. Notch the hidden ends and partitions for the nail rail. The long cut can be made with the tablesaw and rip fence, and the short one with a handsaw.

9. If you will have adjustable shelves, machine the grooves for the shelf standard now with a hand or overarm router and a ⅝-in. bit. I prefer the standard to protrude a little above the surface of the wood; it acts like a bumper so shelves don't scratch the ends or partitions. In most cases, the groove will run from top to bottom, but if you're stopping at a planned point, start the groove at the bottom. Don't bother to square off the top end of the groove (p. 47).

10. If blind dadoes or rabbets are being used, cut away the front edges of the shelves, dust panels or bottom so they'll be flush with the front edges of the ends and partitions. The cut should be the exact depth of the dado, so there won't be a gap between the shelf and end or partition. This cut can be made on the jointer, but first test-cut the joint on scrap and try it in the blind dado.

11. When all the joints have been cut, test-fit the parts. If the bit has been worn away by sharpening, or if some of the shelves and dust panels are too thick, the pieces may not fit into the dadoes. If this is the case, you'll need to make a shallow rabbet on their ends. This is most accurately done on the tablesaw, where the distance between the fence and the blade can be set at exactly the width of the dado. Test the setup on the edge of scrap that is at least as thick as the dado width. Try the rabbeted scrap in the dado, and adjust the fence until the scrap slips into the dado snugly, without being forced. (Too tight a fit and there won't be room for glue during assembly.) Then rabbet the ends of all the necessary pieces.

Confession Time

How many dadoes or rabbets are in the wrong place? All these joints are inside the case, so they can be repaired without ruining the appearance.

Rip a piece of matching solid wood (about ½₂ in. too thick) to fit the misplaced dado. Glue it in place. When the glue has cured, plane the area flush with the plywood. (Sandpaper won't leave a flat surface.)

Fill misplaced rabbets with a solid-wood patch, a little oversized in thickness and width. Glue and nail the patch in place—don't drive the nails home. When the glue has cured, pull out the nails and saw or plane the patch flush.

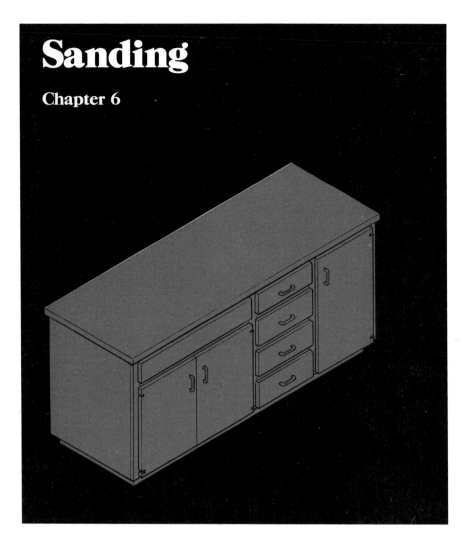

Sanding

Chapter 6

When should you sand and why? How much sanding is necessary? What grit paper should you use? These are some of the questions I'll answer in this chapter; use the chart on the opposite page as a basic guide.

Most sanding should be done before assembly, while the cabinet is still in separate pieces, though final-sanding or a light touch-up is usually necessary after assembly.

For light to medium sanding, I like to use an orbital sander, but it leaves circular scratches, which must be removed from face materials. Some people like to use belt sanders for rough-sanding, but because these sanders cut so fast, they can do extensive damage if not used carefully.

Any sanding will leave minute scratches in the surface of the wood. If the scratches are parallel to the grain they won't show, but if they are at an angle to the grain you'll notice them, especially after the finish has been applied. As a final step, you should always sand face materials along the grain with a straight-line (oscillating) sander or by hand.

When hand-sanding face materials, always use a sanding block. You can buy one, or make your own by stapling or tacking a piece of Naugahide or sheet cork to a ¾-in. by 3-in. by 5½-in. block of wood. A quarter of a standard sheet of sandpaper will fit a block this size.

Most sandpaper is made from one of four abrasives: flint, garnet, aluminum oxide and silicon carbide. I usually use garnet paper, which is hard and tough. Aluminum oxide is good, too, especially for sanding belts. Sandpaper is graded by its coarseness, ranging from 12 grit (extra coarse) to 600 grit (extra fine). For cabinetmaking, most sanding can be done with 80, 100, 120 and 150 grit. Progress from the coarsest grit necessary to the finest, without skipping a grit.

The paper backing on sandpaper is graded by letter: A is lightweight and suitable for light sanding with fine grits; C and D are heavy and durable and should be used with medium to coarse grits. The density of the grit on the paper's surface determines whether a sandpaper is open or closed coat. Open-coat sandpaper has 50 percent to 70 percent of the surface covered, and is less likely to clog than closed-coat paper, which has 100-percent coverage.

Tips on Sanding

Sanding improves the looks of a cabinet by removing water spots, dirt, oil, glue, scratches and mill marks. However, don't rely on sanding to remove more than a small amount of wood—about 1/64 in.

The amount of sanding you need to do can be greatly reduced by keeping your tools sharp and properly adjusted and by handling materials carefully. To avoid scratches, file off sharp corners on machine tables and fences, and keep screws, nails and staples in their containers until they're needed. I use the cabinet back as an auxiliary benchtop, putting it face up on the bench. This way, dents or scratches caused by dried glue or debris on the bench will mar the back face of the piece, where you won't be able to see them.

Glue spills will seal the wood and prevent the finish from penetrating evenly. Some cabinetmakers prefer to wipe up spills with a damp cloth—if you do this, mark the area so that you remember to sand out the water spot after it dries. Other cabinetmakers let the glue set, then remove the dried glue with a sharp knife or chisel, and sand the area.

Keep a light hand when sanding face veneers because they're thin and easy to sand through. When the area begins to change color, you have already gone farther than you should. If the piece is going to receive a dark stain, the error may not be too noticeable. Avoid sanding with dull paper; not only does it waste time, it burnishes the surface of the wood. Burnishing clogs the pores, causing stain to blotch. Also, avoid oversanding fir plywood. This removes the springwood, leaving the harder summerwood raised.

Sanding Guide

	Cabinet Part or Surface	When	Purpose of Sanding	Starting Paper
Visible	Outside of finish end	Before assembly	Remove water spots, dirt, oil, glue, scratches, mill marks, pencil and chalk marks.	Extreme blemishes: 80 grit Medium blemishes: 100 grit Fine blemishes: 120 grit
	Outside of face frame	After	Same as above	Same as above
Visible Sometimes	All inside surfaces visible when doors are open	Before assembly	Remove water spots, dirt, oil, glue pencil and chalk marks, and sharp corners. Fill knotholes, cracks. Small scratches permissible.	Extreme blemishes: 80 grit Medium blemishes: 100 grit
	Inside faces of doors		Same as above	Same as above, to 120 grit.
	Inside edges of face frame	After	Same as above	Same as above, with a block.
Not Visible	Outside of hidden end, back, upper top, partition; underside of lower top and bottom	Before assembly	Remove the worst dirt, oil, glue marks. Scratches, open knots, cracks, mill marks, pencil and chalk marks permissible.	80 grit

Case Assembly

Chapter 7

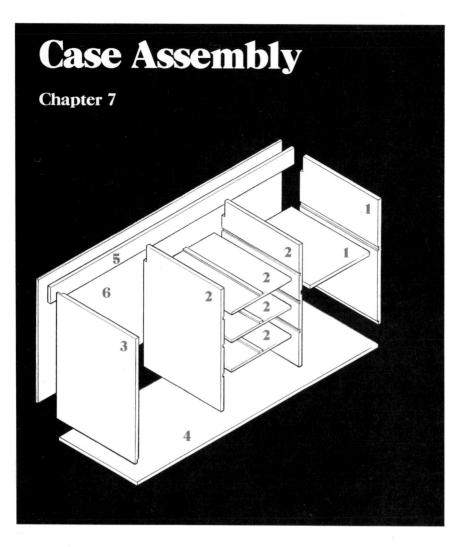

When the parts have been cut to size and edge-banded, the joints made and the initial sanding completed, you're ready to assemble the case. It's natural to reach for the glue bottle and hammer or screwdriver as soon as the parts are ready to go, but haste or impatience now can cause headaches later. Assembly, more than any other facet of cabinetmaking, requires good organization. The parts must go together quickly, before the glue sets; if the assembly is interrupted, it may be impossible to square the case later without breaking some of the joints. This is why it's critical to find the most efficient sequence of assembly *before* glueup, and the best way to do this is by having a dry run. Follow the guidelines on p. 48 for putting the case together—but don't use glue yet.

The case is held together with glue and mechanical fasteners, such as nails, screws or staples. There are a number of glues suitable for case assembly. I find that white glue (polyvinyl acetate) or yellow glue (aliphatic) fill most of my needs. They are easy to apply and clean up, are strong enough for most cabinet work, and don't set so fast that you can't get the case together. The chart on the opposite page lists different types of glue and their characteristics.

Mechanical fasteners draw cabinet parts together and hold them in position while the glue cures. They also reinforce the glue joint—the weaker the joint (on end-grain to end-grain surfaces, for example), the more important the mechanical fastener. I use nails for most of the case, but sometimes I use screws to fasten the nail rail to the ends and partitions. In industry, staples are often used to assemble cabinets, but they are driven into the wood too quickly to draw the parts together. If you use staples to assemble the case, make sure that you clamp the parts together tightly while stapling.

In general, nails (and staples) should be about three times as long as the thickness of the piece through which they are driven. (The case is made of ¼-in., ½-in. and ¾-in.-thick wood, so you'll need nails 1 in., 1½ in. and 2 in. long.) I use finish nails because their small heads are less visible.

Common Glues and Their Characteristics

Characteristics	Aliphatic	Animal Liquid Type	Contact Cement	Plastic Resin	Polyvinyl Acetate	Resorcinol
Pot Life[1]	1 yr.	1½ yr.	1 yr.	½–4 hr.	1 yr.	½–4 hr.
Mixing or Preparation	None	None	None	Mix with water.	None	Mix with catalyst.
Open-Assembly Time[2]	5 min.	10 min.	15–120 min.	5–10 min.	3–5 min.	10–80 min.
Closed-Assembly Time	5–10 min.	15–20 min.	None	10–15 min.	5–10 min.	20–75 min.
Clamping Pressure[3]	25–100 psi	25–200 psi	Roller or hammer and block	50–300 psi	100–250 psi	25–75 psi
Clamping Time	20–120 min.	1–3 hr.	Immediate	12–16 hr.	20–60 min.	1½–8 hr.
Curing Time[4]	72 hr.	12–16 hr.	Up to 30 days	24–48 hr.	8 hr.	12–24 hr.
Gap Filling[5]	Some	Low	Low	Low	Low	Low
Advantages	Can be applied down to 40°F	Very strong, sands well	Doesn't require clamping	Water-resistant, no creep[6]	Dries clear, nonstaining	Waterproof, no creep
Limitations	Softens with heat from belt sander, creep	Not water-resistant	Low strength, creep	Should be applied at 70°F or above	Softens with heat from belt sander, creep	Should be applied at 70°F or above, costly

[1] **Pot Life:** The amount of time glue remains usable after it has been prepared for use.

[2] **Assembly Time:** The amount of time between spreading glue on the surfaces to be joined and applying pressure. Open-assembly time is from the beginning of spreading to joint closure; closed-assembly time is from joint closure to application of full pressure.

[3] **Clamping Pressure:** The amount of pressure applied to a joint, measured in pounds per square inch (PSI).

[4] **Curing Time:** The amount of time between application of full pressure and the joint's achieving maximum strength.

[5] **Gap Filling:** The ability of the glue to contribute strength to a poorly cut joint.

[6] **Creep:** A glue's ability to allow for movement after curing.

Screws draw the parts together and hold them better than nails do, but screws take more time to install. Screws should be long enough so that two-thirds of the screw protrude into the bottom board. You must drill a clearance hole through the top board, or the screw won't draw the two boards tightly together. Use a countersink (or a large drill bit) to make the screwhead flush with the board, or counterdrill to lower the head beneath the surface and fill the hole with a wooden plug. (You can buy plug cutters in ¼-in., ⅜-in., ½-in. and ⅝-in. diameters.) If you are screwing into hardwood, drill a pilot hole, as shown in the drawing below.

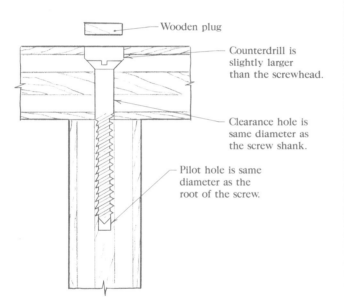

Wooden plug

Counterdrill is slightly larger than the screwhead.

Clearance hole is same diameter as the screw shank.

Pilot hole is same diameter as the root of the screw.

When using screws, always drill a clearance hole in the top board. Drill a pilot hole in hardwood that might split, but you won't need one when screwing into the face of a plywood panel or into softwood.

Furniture makers use clamps instead of mechanical fasteners to draw the parts tightly together until the glue dries. Kitchen cabinets can be glued the same way, but I recommend clamping the pieces together, and then nailing or screwing them. Remove each clamp after the fastener is in place, and you'll need only a few clamps to assemble a whole cabinet. If a joint opens, clamp it until the glue cures.

Clamping

The clamping process is fraught with variables and pitfalls, but for cabinetmakers with the time, patience and equipment, clamping is an excellent way to ensure tight joints. You can use clamps with nails or screws, which position the pieces, or without them. Before beginning to actually glue and clamp the case pieces, dry-clamp to see if you can get everything together—if you can't do this with sufficient speed, the glue may set up before you are finished assembling the case, and then it will be impossible to square the case without breaking glue joints.

Clamp manufacturers do not always agree on the amount of pressure each clamp is capable of exerting, and all craftsmen who turn a clamp handle don't have the same amount of strength. In general, when edge-gluing ¾-in. stock, it's safe to use one bar clamp for each 18 in. to 24 in. of length. Probably the best way to check the pressure (and amount of glue) is to check the glue line: a small bead of glue should run the full length of the joint. When using more than one clamp, tighten them all to exert moderate pressure, then go back and tighten them all down.

Applying even pressure to the entire joint requires some ingenuity at times. Keep in mind that a clamp exerts maximum pressure in an arc of about 45° to an imaginary line drawn between the jaws of the clamp. (This line is the direct line of clamping pressure.) Beyond that arc, the pressure diminishes. Using a backup board will help ensure even pressure, as will using extra clamps— but don't use too many clamps, or you may pull the case out of square.

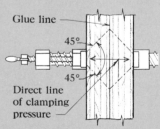

Glue line

45°

45°

Direct line of clamping pressure

Place the clamps carefully, so that they don't distort the squareness of the case. The line of clamping pressure should always be at a right angle to the joint. Be sure to double-check the glued-up assembly to make sure it's square. This step is particularly important if you leave the clamps on while the glue cures; you won't be able to jostle the parts to square them up later.

Before assembly, try to anticipate all the tasks that will be difficult or impossible to do after the case has been put together. Install wooden drawer guides and adjustable shelf standard now and save yourself frustration and scraped knuckles later.

The mating sets of shelf standard should be the same distance from the cabinet bottom. The top of the standard should be flush with or below the top end of the ends and partitions, so that it won't interfere with the placement of the countertop. Some standard has bracket slots numbered 1 through 6: cut the standard so that the numbers are in the same position relative to the bottom on all four pieces. Then you can place brackets at the same height by matching the numbers, rather than by counting slots. (A simple fixture for sawing the standard to length is shown in the drawing below.) Avoid cutting through the holes in the shelf standard; when the holes are cut in half, they leave sharp points, which are likely to scratch cabinet parts and careless people.

If you are attaching one case to another with bolts, you may want to drill those holes now, before assembling each case. Make the holes $\frac{1}{32}$ in. larger than the diameter of the bolts.

All the pieces of metal shelf standard for a set of adjustable shelves should be the same distance from the bottom of the cabinet. Push a piece of scrap against the bottom rabbet for a reliable indexing surface.

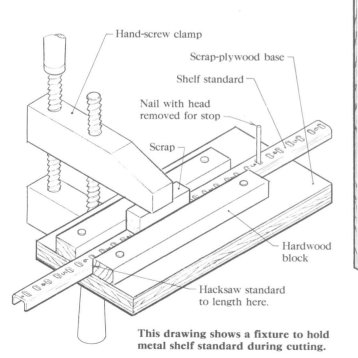

This drawing shows a fixture to hold metal shelf standard during cutting.

Putting the Case Together

During the dry run, decide how to break the case into small units (subassemblies), so it can be assembled in stages and in the most efficient order. Try to think through all the problems that might arise during glueup, too. Are there nails or screws that need to be driven into awkward spots? Is it okay for a nail or screw to show? How will the parts be supported and held in place during assembly? If you need to use several clamps at once, make sure you know how to position them.

Mistakes you might not have noticed earlier will become obvious during the dry run. For example, if the bottom is a little bit short, or if the rabbet into which it fits is too deep, it may be impossible to get the back on in its correct position. (If you don't want to shorten the case, glue a wider piece of solid wood to the end of the bottom; after the glue cures, trim the bottom to the correct length.)

When you're ready to glue up, place the case parts and all the tools and supplies you'll need close by. Make up the subassemblies first. (In the case below, the joints are numbered to show the order in which they are put together.)

1. Glue and nail the fixed shelf to the hidden end. Use a stick of wood, a brush or your finger to spread the glue evenly in the dado, up the sides as well as on the bottom. Because this is a hidden end, you can nail through it into the shelf. For a finish end, toenail

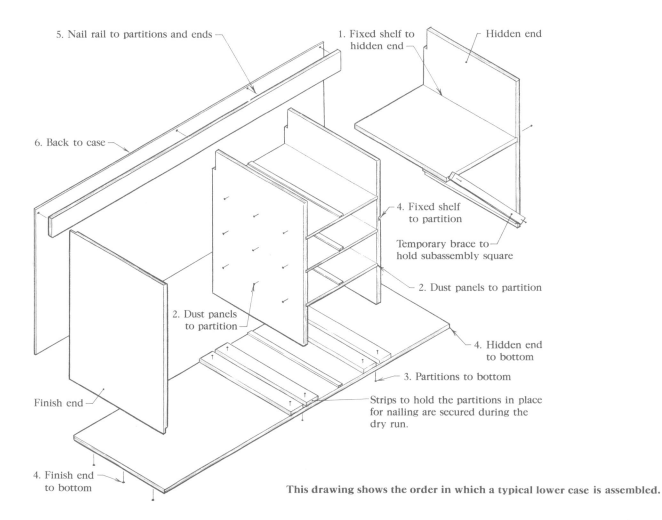

5. Nail rail to partitions and ends

1. Fixed shelf to hidden end

Hidden end

6. Back to case

4. Fixed shelf to partition

Temporary brace to hold subassembly square

2. Dust panels to partition

2. Dust panels to partition

4. Hidden end to bottom

3. Partitions to bottom

Strips to hold the partitions in place for nailing are secured during the dry run.

Finish end

4. Finish end to bottom

This drawing shows the order in which a typical lower case is assembled.

the shelf so the nail will be hidden, as shown in the drawing below. Before the glue sets, check both faces of the shelf for squareness to the hidden end. A scrap brace secures the pieces while the glue cures.

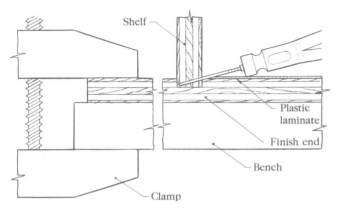

Toenail a shelf to a finish end so the nails won't show. Plastic laminate prevents the hammer from marring the end. Use a nail set to drive in the last ¼ in. of the nail.

2. Make up the center subassembly next. Spread glue in the dadoes on both partitions, and insert the dust panels. If you nail through the partitions, you can place one of them on the bench while you nail through the other. While nailing, try to hold the dust panels square to the partitions to get a tight joint. Check the subassembly for square by measuring the diagonals between dust panels—measuring to the ends of the partition isn't reliable because nothing keeps them from running wild. When the diagonals are equal, the subassembly is square. Tack on a brace to hold it square, if necessary.

3. Glue and nail the center subassembly to the bottom. The partitions are butt-jointed to the bottom and must be secured for nailing—nail or clamp strips of wood on each side of the partitions for support. (Remove the strips once the bottom is nailed on.)

4. Attach the hidden-end subassembly and the finish end, clamping them in place while nailing through the bottom. Move the clamp as nailing progresses, to get by using only one clamp.

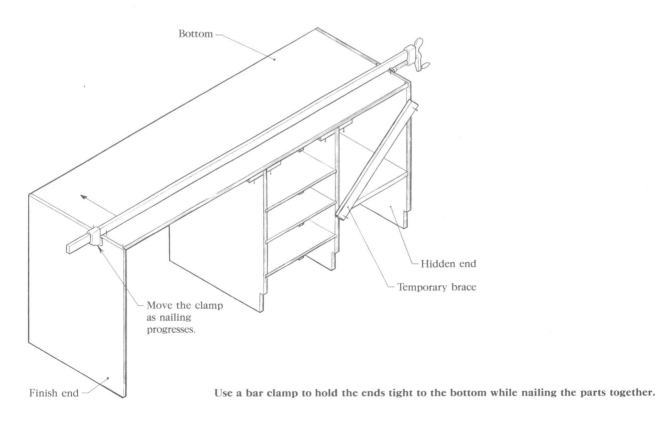

Use a bar clamp to hold the ends tight to the bottom while nailing the parts together.

5. The nail rail is next. Roll the case onto its face carefully, trying not to rack the joints. Lay the rail along the bottom and mark the position of each partition and end on it, as shown in the upper drawing below. Glue and nail the rail in place, aligning each vertical piece under its mark. (Because the nail rail of an upper case carries most of the cabinet's weight, I sometimes fasten this piece with screws.)

6. Check the back to make sure that it fits. The back is the most important structural part of the cabinet. It must have at least one square corner, and the case must be squared to that corner. If only one edge of the back is straight, be sure to use it along the bottom of the case.

7. Glue and nail the back in place, as shown in the lower drawing below. Make certain you put the good

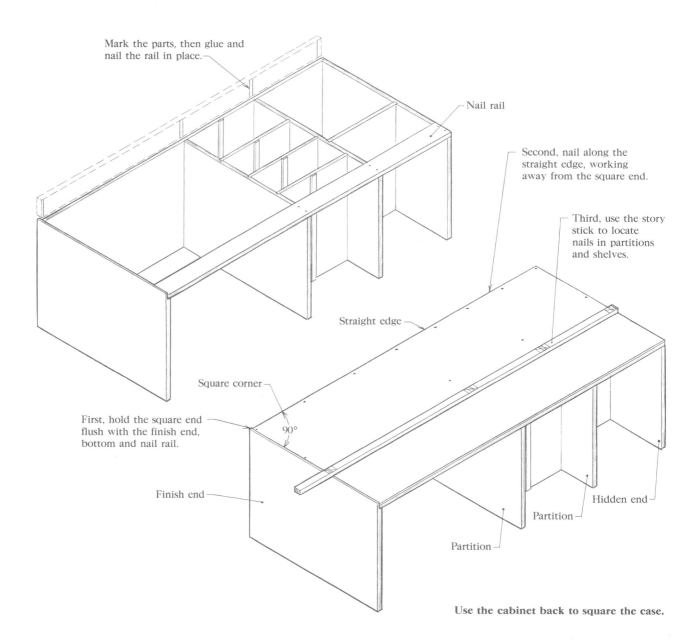

Mark the parts, then glue and nail the rail in place.

Nail rail

Second, nail along the straight edge, working away from the square end.

Third, use the story stick to locate nails in partitions and shelves.

Straight edge

Square corner

90°

First, hold the square end flush with the finish end, bottom and nail rail.

Finish end

Hidden end

Partition

Partition

Use the cabinet back to square the case.

face of the back on the inside of the case, where it will show. Spread glue on the back edge of all the case parts. Hold the square end of the back against the allowance for scribing on the finish end or flush with a hidden end, and nail with 2d box nails or staples spaced every 12 in. If you're stapling the back on, make sure it's pushed tightly against the case before driving in the staples.

8. Align the bottom of the case with the bottom edge of the back, and nail or staple it down, working away from the end that's just been nailed. This should pull the case square.

9. Now nail or staple the back to the other parts, using the horizontal and vertical sticks to locate them. Then go back and put nails or staples at 3-in. or 4-in. intervals.

10. After the case is assembled, and before moving onto the second phase of construction, there are two more things to do. First, slightly round the corners on the top and bottom ends of the hidden and finish ends to prevent the face veneer from chipping off.

(The corners on the edges of the finish ends should be sharp for a good fit with the face frame or wall.)

Second, make and attach skids to the bottoms of the lower cases and the tops of the upper cases to protect them and to make them easier to move around the shop. (The skids can be left in place until the cabinets have been delivered to the site and are ready to be installed.) Make the skids from ¾-in. stock about 1½ in. wide and 2 in. longer than the case. After cutting the skids to size, bevel their ends with a bandsaw, disc sander, handsaw or plane; nail them to the bottom of the case, front and back, with the ends protruding about 1 in.

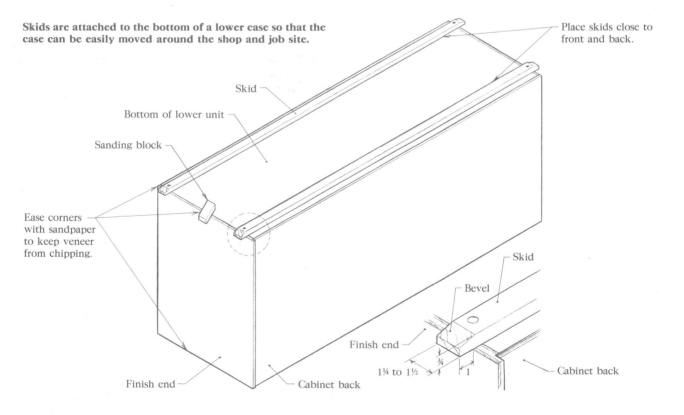

Skids are attached to the bottom of a lower case so that the case can be easily moved around the shop and job site.

Place skids close to front and back.

Skid

Bottom of lower unit

Sanding block

Ease corners with sandpaper to keep veneer from chipping.

Skid

Bevel

Finish end

1¼ to 1½   ¾   1

Finish end

Cabinet back

Cabinet back

Face Frames

Chapter 8

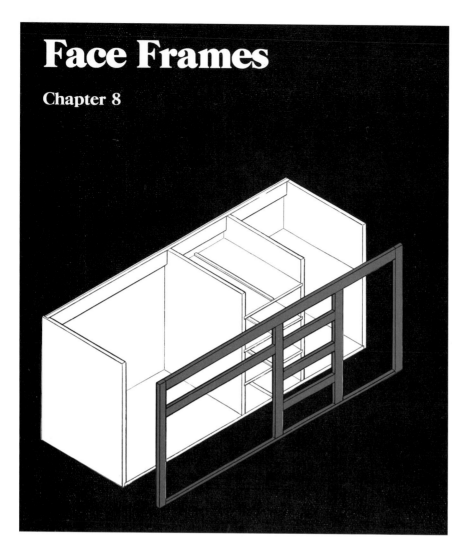

When the case has been assembled, you can begin the second phase of cabinetmaking—building the face frame. The face frame is made from knot-free, straight-grained, solid wood of the same species as the face veneer of the cabinet. The frame is held together with glue and dowels, then attached to the front of the case with nails and glue. Although they are a good way to hide the raw edges of plywood case parts, face frames are not a requirement: lip, flush and overlay door and drawer faces can all be used with or without a face frame, as shown in the drawing on the opposite page.

Here are some criteria to keep in mind when designing face frames. It's important to try to hide the end grain of all the parts of the frame that will be visible. End grain isn't pretty, and because it soaks up more finish than edge or face grain, it will appear darker than the rest of the frame after finishing. For example, run the top rails between end stiles and over the tops of any intermediate stiles. Bottom rails can be made of either one long piece of wood, or a series of short rails fitted between the stiles. The drawing on the opposite page shows both ways of making a bottom rail, but whichever method you choose, be consistent and use it on all your cabinets. Of course, you won't need to have a bottom rail if door or drawer faces are going to cover the cabinet bottom. If you choose not to have a bottom rail, however, you should edge-band the cabinet bottom to hide the plies of the plywood.

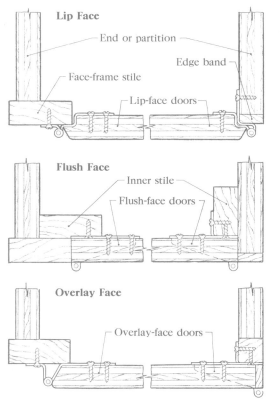

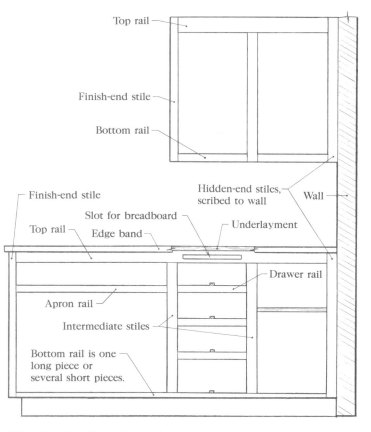

Decide whether or not to use face frames before laying out the story sticks. Lip, flush and overlay door and drawer faces can all be used with or without a face frame.

Hide all end-grain surfaces of visible face-frame parts. The stile bottoms are below eye level, so it's okay to leave end grain exposed.

When to Use Face Frames

As I discussed on p. 14, you must decide whether or not to use face frames before laying out the story sticks. Take these factors into account when making your decision:

Appearance—Plywood edges can be hidden with either solid-wood banding or a solid-wood face frame. For an outline wider than ¾ in. around the doors and drawers, use a face frame.

Scribing allowance—The edge of a face-frame stile can be fitted to the contours of an irregular wall. Without a face frame, getting a close fit is practically impossible, but you can get around this by attaching a recessed stile (about 1¼ in. wide) to the hidden end, and scribing the stile to the wall. A recessed stile will also keep drawer faces (particularly, overlay faces) from dragging along the wall as the drawer is pulled out. (If you don't want to use a recessed stile or a face frame, don't put drawers at the cabinet's wall end.)

Hinges—Many hinges can be mounted either on the edges of cabinet ends and partitions or on face-frame stiles. Some hinges won't mount on the edge of a partition or end, and must be used with a face frame. The width of the flange that mounts to the face frame will determine the stile width. It's important to select all hardware before laying out the cabinets, so you can plan on stiles wide enough to provide the necessary mounting surface.

The width of face-frame rails and stiles is somewhat dependent on individual taste, though certain relationships of the parts to one another are standard. For example, the top rail is usually the widest part. On upper cabinets, top rails 3 in. or 4 in. wide are quite common; wider rails may be used to keep the door sizes practical for cutting. On lower cabinets, the top rail is usually about 2½ in. wide to allow for a 1¼-in.-wide countertop edge band and a ⅞-in. breadboard opening. (A top rail any wider than this wouldn't do anything but rob valuable drawer space.) Other rails, such as apron rails and rails over dust panels and fixed shelves, should be no wider than the top rail, and usually they are narrower. Sometimes, rails as narrow as 1 in. are used.

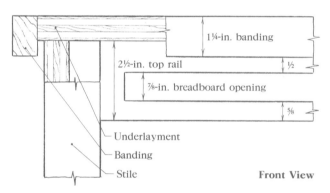

A lower cabinet's top rail is about 2½ in. wide, to allow for the breadboard opening and countertop edge band.

If the bottom of an upper cabinet is rabbeted into the ends, the bottom rail will be only ¾ in. wide. If the bottom is dadoed into the ends, the rail will have to be wide enough to cover the bottom and the ends. Bottom rails on lower cabinets are typically ¾ in. wide—if you think the cabinet will look better with a wider bottom rail, remember that the bottom of the cabinet must be flush with the top of the rail.

The face-frame stiles at the end of a flush-face cabinet should be the same width or wider than the intermediate stiles. If the intermediate stiles are overlapped by door or drawer faces on both edges, you'll have to widen them to make all the stiles appear the same width. Lip-face doors and drawers overlap the stiles ¼ in.; overlay faces overlap ¹³⁄₆₄ in. to ¾ in., depending on the hinges used. The face of a beveled overlay door hides ⅝ in. of the stile. (When using a beveled overlay door or drawer face, be sure that you leave enough room on the intermediate stiles for two side-by-side hinges. Because these doors and drawers are often used without pulls, you should also leave enough room between their faces for a person's finger to hook around.)

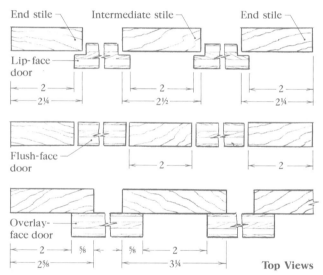

The stiles on lip-face and overlay-face doors will appear to be the same width because the intermediate stile is made wider to compensate for being overlapped by two doors.

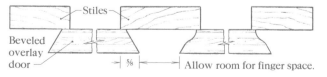

This drawing shows two variations of beveled overlay doors. To use them without pulls, leave enough room between the faces for a person's finger to hook the edge.

Building the Face Frame

1. Rough-cut the wood into single or multiple lengths 1 in. to 2 in. longer than finish length. Then plane the wood to between ¾ in. and $1\frac{3}{16}$ in. thick.

2. Joint one edge of each piece square to the faces. With the jointed edge against the tablesaw fence, rip the parts $\frac{1}{16}$ in. wider than finish width.

3. Now joint the sawn edge of all the parts to exact width in one cut. The width of the bottom rail, if you have one, is critical, so check it carefully against the cabinet bottom.

4. Rough-cut the rails and stiles 1 in. longer than finished length. Save the scrap from each part and label it—you'll need the scraps later. Make sure the end you cut is square to the edges of the board, and mark that end as well.

5. Often, a face frame will require two or more short rails to be the same length (for example, in a stack of drawers). Use the cutoff box and a stop block to cut all the rails in a set exactly the same. If sets of these rails extend all the way across the case, cut all but one set to length now. Cut the last set on the setup described in step 7, to compensate for minor errors and to ensure exact overall face-frame length.

To finish-cut the rest of the rails and stiles, use the following method, which will save setup time and ensure accuracy. You'll be able to do the job in two or three setups on the cutoff box—one or two for the rails and one for the stiles.

6. To set up the cut for the top and bottom rails, clamp a stop block on the cutoff box at a distance from the blade equal to the overall length of the face frame. Make a test cut on a piece of scrap, then check the length of the scrap against the horizontal stick and the case. (Slight errors in case length are corrected when scribing, so the face frame is made as it is laid out on the stick.) However, if both ends are finish ends, set the stop to $\frac{1}{32}$ in. longer than the cabinet, so that the stiles can be planed or sanded flush with the cabinet ends.

The top and bottom rails must be as long as the overall length of the face frame, minus the width of the stiles at each end. Hold two scraps of end stile (one scrap from each) against the stop, and put the square (marked) end of the top rail against the scrap. When the rail is properly positioned, hold it in place against the push bar of the cutoff box and let the scraps fall away. Then cut the rail to length. Cut the bottom rail the same way.

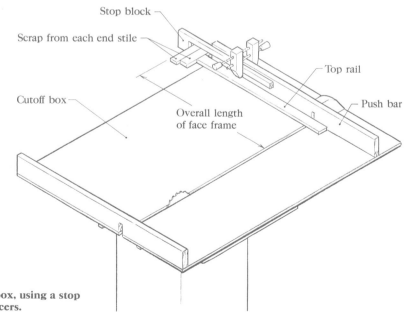

Cut the top and bottom rails on the cutoff box, using a stop block and a scrap of each end stile for spacers.

7. If the case has short rails extending all the way across its face, cut the last set of them on the same setup. Put a finish-cut short rail from each of the other sets against the stop block, then a scrap of each end stile and scraps of all intermediate stiles. Position the square end of the last rail to be cut against these pieces to make the cut. (The setup below is for a case having two sets of short rails.)

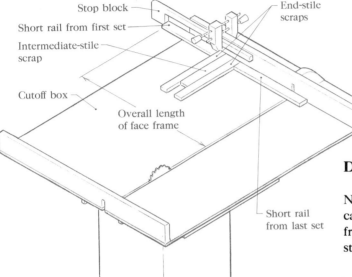

If sets of short rails extend across the case, cut the last set using face-frame scraps for positioning, to ensure accurate face-frame length.

8. Another setup will allow you to cut the stiles to length. Clamp a stop block on the cutoff box to the overall height of the frame. Make a test cut and check it against the vertical stick and the case. Cut the end stiles first, holding the square end of each stile against the stop block.

9. Cut the intermediate stiles with scraps from the top and bottom rail (if there is a bottom rail) against the stop block.

10. The stile on the hidden end is ¼ in. wider than the other stiles to allow for scribing it to the wall. If you rabbet this allowance, as shown in the drawing above at right, there will be less wood to cut away when scribing. (On an upper unit, stop the rabbet about ½ in. from the bottom end so it won't show.) If

you cut this rabbet now, fill it out with a block under the clamp when gluing up the face frame, or you won't get even pressure and may crush the rabbet.

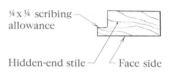

Rabbet the stiles that will be scribed to a wall, so there will be less wood to remove when scribing.

Doweling and Assembling the Face Frame

Now it's time to dowel the face frame together. Some cabinetmakers use mortise-and-tenon joints in their frames, but the dowel joint is easier to make and strong enough for the job.

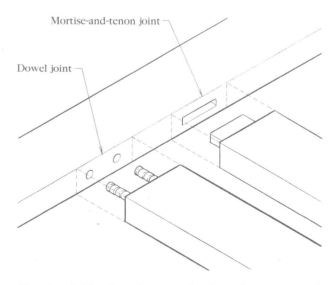

The dowel joint is easier to make than the mortise-and-tenon joint, and strong enough to use in a face frame.

Drilling holes in wood at a right angle to the surface, precisely where you want them, can be a difficult operation. The grain of the wood will frequently cause the drill bit to shift, and it is often hard to hold the drill perpendicular to the surface. Two pieces of equipment will help you deal with these problems. The first is the proper drill bit. I use a center-spur wood bit with a power drill or an auger bit with a brace; both of these are less likely to shift than a standard twist-drill bit. The second piece of equipment is a doweling jig. A doweling jig helps align holes, prevents shifting of the bit and ensures the holes are drilled at a right angle to the surface. A number of different jigs are available, and each requires its own marking system. (For best results, follow the instructions that come with your jig.) For dowels, I recommend using hardwood spiral dowels that are 5/16 in. or 3/8 in. in diameter and 2 in. long.

1. Begin by laying out the parts of the frame on the bench just as they will go together. Then hold the end stile against the assembled case and mark the position of the bottom directly on it, as shown in the drawing below. (This gives the position of the bottom rail, which must be flush with the top face of the cabinet bottom.) Mark the position of each dust panel directly on the appropriate stiles, holding them in place against the case. (This gives the position of the top edges of the rails over the dust panels.) Clamp the top rail in place on the case to position the intermediate stiles for marking.

2. Now study the frame to determine the order in which the joints should be assembled. This is an important step, because once you begin assembly, glueup must progress without delay, or else you risk the glue curing before assembly is complete. Each frame is a puzzle with its own solution, but in general, it's best to start the assembly in the center and work outward—if you work toward the center, you may have trouble fitting the last rails in place. Mark the joints to show the order of assembly, as shown in the drawing below. A sketch of the face frame should be marked in the same way to avoid confusion if the parts get mixed up.

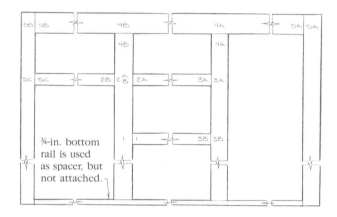

Number mating pieces of each joint according to their order of assembly before you drill the dowel holes.

3. Drill the dowel holes about 1/8 in. deeper than half the dowel length. Try to use two dowels at each joint. Placing them as far apart as possible will increase strength and reduce twisting. Also, try to center the dowels on the board's edge. If the cabinet's bottom rail is 3/4 in. wide, don't dowel it; it gets glued to the stiles when the frame is attached to the case.

4. After drilling, shake out the shavings and check that the holes are deep enough. A hole that is too shallow is a disaster during assembly—the frame just won't go together. Then put the frame on the bench again and check that you've drilled all the holes. Don't attempt dry assembly—the dowels fit so tightly, there's a risk of them breaking during disassembly.

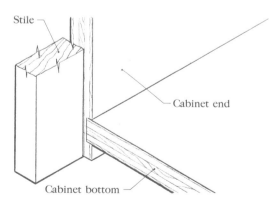

In a cabinet with a dadoed bottom, the bottom rail of the face frame must align with the bottom. Mark the bottom directly on the stile, so you'll know where to dowel.

5. Now gather the materials you'll need for glueup: glue, a small brush, bar clamps, clamp pads, hammer and dowels. If the cabinet is to be fitted between two walls, leave one end stile loose, so that it can be scribed to fit the wall and glued on at the job site. Remember that each dowel joint has one piece of end grain meeting a piece of edge grain. Glue dowels only into end-grain holes before assembling the frame; this way, you won't wind up with a joint having four dowels and no holes.

6. Spread a good film of glue on the end-grain surface of the rail or stile with your finger or a small brush, putting a bead of glue just inside and at the top of the dowel hole. Don't pour glue into the bottom of the hole because it won't compress when the dowel is inserted, and the piece may split.

7. Coat each dowel with glue and then tap it gently into the end-grain hole with a hammer until no more than 1 in. protrudes.

8. Next, put a good film of glue around the edge-grain hole in the mating piece. Start the dowel into the hole and then draw the joint together with a clamp, padding the jaws of the clamp to prevent damage to the frame parts. Never hammer the parts together, because it's too easy to break the dowels. When the joint is tight, tiny beads of glue will show that you've used the right amount. If no glue shows along the joint, you may not have used enough, or maybe you didn't get the clamps on fast enough; if there's a lot of glue along the joint, it means that you've used too much.

9. Progress to the next joint. By the time it's ready for a clamp, it will probably be okay to remove the previous clamp. The glue doesn't take long to set, and the joint will remain tight as long as no strain is put on it. Work rapidly through the entire frame, doing one or two joints at a time. The last two parts to join to the assembly are usually the end stiles. (Remember to leave one loose if the cabinet must fit between two walls.)

10. When the frame is assembled, check that the joints are tight, reclamping as necessary. Check the frame for square by measuring its diagonals, and reposition any clamps before the glue sets, if necessary. It's okay for the frame to be out of square by ⅛ in. or less, because this much of an error can be corrected when the frame is attached to the cabinet.

11. After the glue has cured, sand the faces of the pieces flush at the joints. If more than ¹⁄₆₄ in. needs to be removed, use a hand plane and then sand. Final-sanding can be done after the frame is attached to the case.

12. Now lay out and cut the opening for the breadboard in the top rail. Add ⅛ in. to the thickness and width of the breadboard to determine the size of the opening. (See p. 80 for how to make a breadboard.) You can cut the opening with a tablesaw, but because the sawblade is round, the cut goes further on the bottom face of the rail than the top. You have to gauge the length of the cut from the bottom of the piece or else you'll cut too far. Here's how to do it.

Raise the sawblade to its full height and mark the table where the blade intersects the tabletop. Transfer these marks to the fence. Adjust the fence to cut the lower edge of the breadboard opening. (Remember the kerf must fall in the waste.) Make a test cut in a piece of scrap and check it on the layout lines.

Lower the blade and put the frame on the saw, aligning the marks farthest from you on the fence and rail. Hold the frame securely, turn the saw on and raise the blade to its maximum height. Move the frame forward until the second set of marks are in line. Turn off the saw and remove the frame.

Adjust the fence to cut the top edge of the opening and repeat the cutting operation.

A handsaw and chisel will be required to finish the kerf and cut the ends of the opening. Square the ends with a chisel.

13. Before attaching the face frame to the case, decide whether you want to hide the joint or accent it

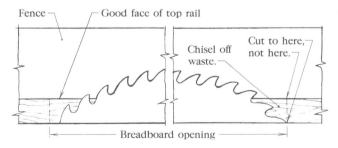

The blade cuts further on the bottom face of a board than on the top. Raise the blade as high as it will go and mark the table and fence where the blade intersects the tabletop.

where the frame meets the finish end. An inconspicuous joint requires that the end stile and the finish end be perfectly aligned, so you may need to plane and sand the face frame after attaching it to the case.

Accenting the joint with a quirk is a good way to hide imperfect alignment. Cut the quirk before attaching the face frame to the case. It can be cut square or in the shape of a *V.* Make the *V*-quirk with a few strokes of a hand plane on the corner of both the frame and finish end. You can saw the square quirk on the face-frame stile before assembling the frame. Or rout it on the finish end, using a router mounted in an edge-banding trimmer, after the case is assembled. (See p. 119 for how to build a trimmer.)

Attaching the Face Frame to the Case

Before you begin, make sure any adjustable shelves will fit through the frame openings. Sometimes, shelves must be installed before nailing on the frame.

1. The upper front corners of the ends and partitions are loose, so tack the horizontal story stick in place on the case to restrain them. Align each vertical piece under its corresponding mark on the stick.

2. Spread a thin film of glue on the front edges of the case. Too much glue on the outside edge of the finish end will squeeze into the quirk (if there is one).

3. Put the frame on the case and nail the stile to the finish end, using four or five 5d finish nails. Try to get the edge of the stile flush with the face of the end. Then put a nail through the top rail into each partition—make sure that they are flush at the top, and the bottom rail is in place. Nail the stile to the other end; on a hidden end, there should be some overhang for scribing to the wall. A cabinet that fits between two walls will have one unattached stile; attach the loose end of each rail to the cabinet end with a strip of wood (p. 98).

4. Nail the intermediate stiles. Intermediate rails can be held tightly against the fixed shelf or dust panel with a nail or two. Lastly, nail the bottom rail in place. (A ¾-in. bottom rail will be loose, so make sure it's positioned accurately.)

5. Check to be sure that the face frame is drawn in tightly to the case, especially at the finish end. Close any gaps with a nail or bar clamp before the glue sets. Set all nails approximately ¹⁄₁₆ in. below the surface of the wood. After the glue has set, plane and sand the frame flush to the finish end (if no quirk is used). Sand the entire frame and dull all the corners, except the scribe. (Sharp corners will dent easily and don't feel good to the touch.)

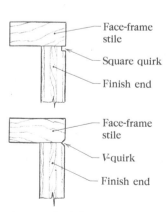

Accent the joint between the finish end and the face frame with a square or *V*-quirk.

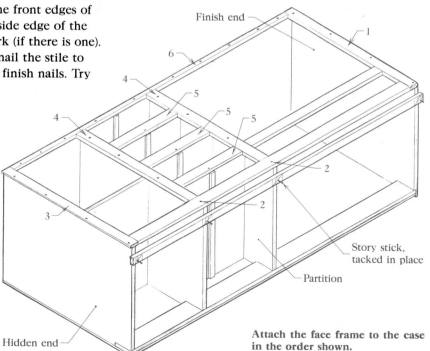

Attach the face frame to the case in the order shown.

Door and Drawer Faces

Chapter 9

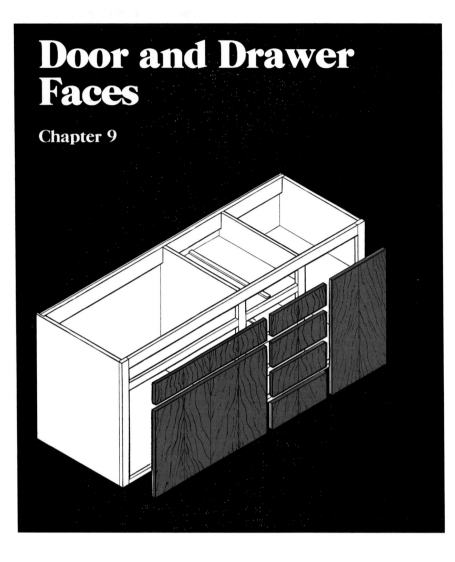

Once you've fastened the face frame to the case, you're ready to cut out the door and drawer faces. Though you've already chosen the material (plywood or solid wood) and style of the faces (lip, overlay or flush), you must still decide how best to use the grain patterns of the wood.

It's a good idea to chalk out all the faces at once. Choose sheets of plywood with similar color and grain for units in the same part of the kitchen, and try to get all the face parts for one cabinet out of the same sheet. When laying out, divide the face for each cabinet into vertical sections (consisting of, for example, a stack of drawers or a sink-apron face and pair of doors), which can then be rough-cut into easy-to-handle blanks. The individual parts are cut to final

dimension from the blanks later on. Run the grain of face parts vertically. I think the widest part of the grain pattern looks best at the bottom of lower units and at the top of uppers.

When laying out each vertical section, try to center the grain pattern in the middle of a door or stack of drawers, or on the split between a pair of doors. It's easy to center the grain on book-matched plywood because the grain is symmetrical around the glue lines. If there is more than one glue line, mark the one you'll be using as the centerline for easy reference when machining the parts. The glue lines should run perpendicular to the width of the face, otherwise the cabinet will seem to lean. It's more difficult to center rotary-cut plywood because the grain of the face veneer is not symmetrical around the glue lines, as it is in book-matched plywood. Try to arrange the grain on rotary-cut plywood parts so the cabinet doesn't look lopsided. Chalk in very light centerlines on each part, perpendicular to the width of the face. Using the story sticks, position the part and chalk its outline.

When chalking out the parts, keep in mind that lip faces cover ¼ in. of the face frame and overlay faces cover $^{13}/_{64}$ in. to ¾ in. (depending on the hinges used); both these types of faces must be larger all around than the face-frame openings. Remember the craftsman's adage: Measure twice and cut once. Face material is expensive, and one wrong cut can ruin an entire sheet, particularly if you're trying to match the grain in a certain way.

The initial steps for cutting out face parts are the same, regardless of the style of the face. I'll discuss these steps before explaining the processes specific to cutting each style.

1. After laying out and chalking the parts on the plywood, rough-cut the blanks. First, rip the long parts (such as toeboards, if you haven't already cut them, or a broom-closet door). The rest of the parts finish no longer than 31¼ in., so now crosscut the sheet into 32-in.-long blanks.

Because there will be some tear-out where the sawblade exits the wood, always be sure that you saw with the good face of the wood turned up. Tear-out is usually minor when ripping, but it can get to be a real problem when crosscutting. Experiment with different blades to find the best way to keep tear-out under control. I find that using a 10-in. carbide blade with 60 or more teeth will usually eliminate tear-out, though sometimes a fine-toothed plywood blade will do a better job.

2. If the glue lines on book-matched plywood (or the centerlines on rotary-cut plywood) aren't parallel to at least one edge of the blank, you'll have to correct this before cutting out the individual faces. Make a small mark on the top and bottom end of the blank, parallel to the glue lines, as shown in the drawing at right. Lay the blank on the cutoff box so that these marks line up over the saw kerf. Place a wedge between the blank and push bar to keep the blank in position, and make the cut. Mark the edge and make the next cuts indexing from the mark.

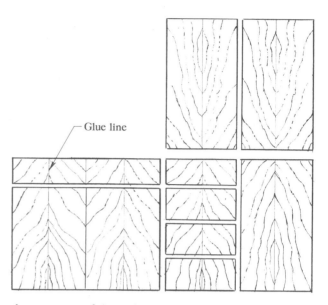

Glue line

Arrangement of the grain on the faces is important. Center the pattern on individual doors, stacks of drawers and on the mating edges of a pair of doors. The widest part of the pattern looks best at the bottom on lower units and at the top on upper units.

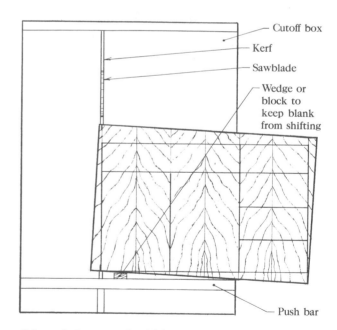

Cutoff box
Kerf
Sawblade
Wedge or block to keep blank from shifting
Push bar

Edges of the parts should be parallel to the glue line on book-matched plywood, or the face will appear to lean. Cut one edge of the blank parallel using the cutoff box before cutting the parts to width.

3. Now rip the parts from each blank to exact width. Remember to check the placement of the centerlines in relation to the cut. Double-check against the story stick—remember that the final width and length of parts with lip or overlay faces will be greater than the dimensions of their openings. Flush faces should fit the opening with no clearance. On flush-face cabinets, the blank that contains the sink-apron face and doors should be ripped one saw kerf wider than the face-frame opening. This way, after the sink-apron face has been cut off and the blank has been ripped in half, the two doors will fit the face-frame opening exactly.

4. Now trim the top end of each part square to the edge, using the cutoff box. You shouldn't assume that the ends are square to the edges until you've either cut them on the cutoff box or checked them with a framing square. Check flush-face parts in the face frame—if the frame is out of square, trim the parts to fit. Then cut off the top-drawer face and the sink-apron face. (You can use the cutoff box or rip fence on the tablesaw.)

5. Cut the remaining drawer faces off the blank and rip the part of the blank under the sink-apron face into two doors. Use the tablesaw and rip fence to make these cuts.

6. Cut doors and bottom drawers to length. If the face frame doesn't have a bottom rail, the doors and bottom drawers will be longer and should align with the bottom edge of the stiles. (If the face frame on a flush-face cabinet has no bottom rail, the doors and bottom drawers are cut to length later.) Mark all parts with chalk so they can be easily identified.

Lip Faces

Doors and drawers with lip faces protrude from the face frame by about ⅜ in. and overlap the frame by about ¼ in. Rabbet only the ends and edges that overlap the face frame, or overlap the edges of a case without a face frame. (Remember that the edge of a board always runs parallel to the face grain; the end is at right angles to it.) If the face-frame rails are narrow, you may want to eliminate the lip on the bottom of the drawer face; if you do this, remember the length of the face should be only ¼ in. more than the height of its opening. A common mistake is to put a lip on the edge of a door where it meets another door—to avoid error, mark where lips should and should not be. Don't rabbet the bottom end of doors or bottom drawers for face frames without a bottom rail. It is critical that the standard ⅜-in. inset hinge fit the rabbet, so buy the hinges before rabbeting.

There are several ways to cut the ⅜-in. by ⅜-in. rabbets. To rout them you'll need a 1-HP router (or larger), a ¾-in. straight bit with two or more carbide-tipped flutes, and a shaper table. Cut the rabbets in one pass—raise the bit ⅜ in. above the table, and then clamp a straightedge to the table so that it covers all but ⅜ in. of the bit. This is a hefty cut, so feed the work steadily and quickly without making the router work too hard. Don't stop the cut midway or you'll burn the wood.

If you are using a tablesaw, set it up as shown in the drawing below, so that you can make both cuts without repositioning the blade or the fence. Make the first cut with the piece on edge, and the good

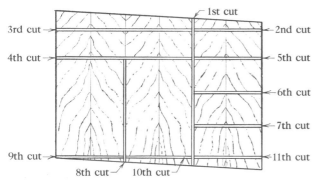

Cut out the face parts in the order shown here.

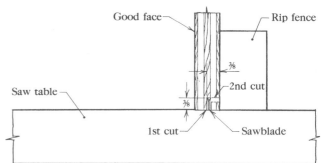

You can cut the rabbets for lip faces on the tablesaw.

face away from the fence. Make this same cut in each end or edge, as necessary.

For the second cut, work with the good face up. Hold the work tightly against the fence, and use a push stick to push the small sliver of waste through the saw to keep it from kicking back.

The edges of lip-face doors and drawers may be left square, bullnosed or chamfered. Leaving them square is simplest—ease sharp corners with sandpaper.

A bullnosed lip is rounded to a ¼-in. radius with a router bit and pilot. This lip style is often used on solid-wood or painted faces. (On plywood with a transparent finish, a bullnose will make the glue lines too obvious.) Don't use a bullnose on the mating edges of a pair of doors, because this would create a deep V-groove; ease these corners with sandpaper only. If you choose to bullnose the lip, do it before rabbeting. After rabbeting, there won't be any wood for the pilot of the router bit to bear against.

Chamfering the lip at a 10° to 20° angle can be done either before or after rabbeting. Chamfered lips are popular on cabinets with transparent finishes because they look more finished than square lips, but don't expose as many glue lines as bullnosed lips.

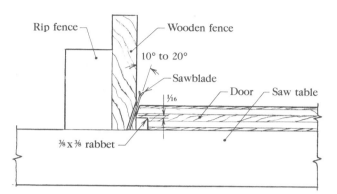

When chamfering the lip, use a temporary wooden fence, screwed or clamped to the rip fence of the tablesaw.

Overlay Faces

An overlay door, drawer or sink-apron face should overlap the opening by $^{13}/_{64}$ in. or ¾ in., depending on the style of hinge used. Cut the overlay-face parts to final dimension following the six steps discussed on pp. 61-62. Overlay faces can be beveled or banded. Beveling the edges eliminates the need for door and drawer pulls because you can open the door by hooking your fingers on the bevel. (The face-frame rails and stiles must be wide enough to allow room for fingers between the faces.) The 60° bevel also hides the plywood plies and glue lines, because the edges slant back behind the face. Bevel the edges using the tablesaw, set up with a wooden fence, as shown in the drawing below. (Remember to place the part on the table with its good face up.)

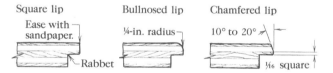

Leave the lip square, bullnose it with a router, or chamfer it on the tablesaw.

To chamfer on the tablesaw, use the setup shown in the drawing above at right. Clamp or screw a wooden fence to the rip fence. With the blade below the table and tilted, and the fence set to the estimated position, turn on the machine and raise the blade up through the wooden fence. Make a test cut in scrap to check the setup. If the rabbet has been precut, about ¹⁄₁₆ in. of the lip must be left square for support against the fence. A 10-in., 60-tooth carbide blade or an 8-in., fine-toothed plywood blade will make a relatively smooth cut requiring minimal sanding.

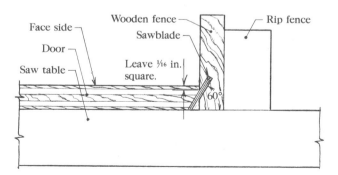

Bevel an overlay door on the tablesaw.

Banding the door and drawer faces also hides the plywood plies and glue lines, but the edges remain square. Banded overlay faces can be used with or without a face frame. The bandings are made from solid wood that matches the face veneer of the plywood and is slightly thicker. They should be ¼ in. to ½ in. wide. Narrower bandings are difficult to glue in place and don't provide as much solid wood for anchoring screws; wider ones are more difficult to trim flush with the face of the plywood. The method used to cut these bands is the same as the one used for making the bands that cover the raw edges of the plywood case (p. 30).

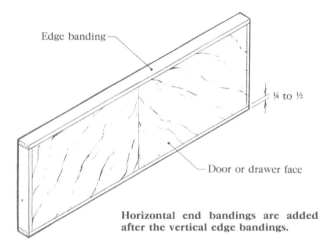

Edge banding

¼ to ½

Door or drawer face

Horizontal end bandings are added after the vertical edge bandings.

Before applying the bandings, rip the door and drawer faces to finish width minus two bandings. Be sure to keep the glue lines centered. Glue the bands on both edges of the door and drawer faces, jointed face out. (The horizontal bands are applied last, to cover the end grain of the vertical bandings.)

After the glue has set, use a hand plane or a router with an edge-band trimmer to make the bandings flush with the faces. Trim the top ends of the parts square in the cutoff box, then cut them to length (finish length minus two bandings).

Now glue bandings to both ends of each part. When the glue has set, trim the extra length off so the ends are flush with the edge bands, then plane or rout the bandings on the ends flush with the plywood faces. Sand the parts, easing the sharp corners.

Flush Faces

On flush-face cabinets, faces of the doors and drawers are flush with the face frame. Flush faces require a higher degree of craftsmanship than lip or overlay faces because the doors and drawers must be accurately fitted in their openings for an even clearance between the face and the frame.

Cut out the flush-face parts following the six steps on pp. 61-62. The faces should fit tightly in their face-frame openings. (If any pairs of doors are still in one piece, split them on the tablesaw.) Now you need to make sure the doors will have the correct amount of clearance and are beveled to swing easily.

Clearance allowance and bevel angle can be cut at the same time on the jointer. Set the fence at 85° to the table and set the infeed table so that ¹⁄₃₂ in. or less will be removed from the edges and ends of the doors. Most fences tilt both ways, but if you tilt the fence at an acute rather than an obtuse angle, the piece is less likely to slip when you push down on it.

Joint the ends and edges of each door and drawer face. The clearance should be uniform around the face, about a dime's worth at each edge and end. For a pair of doors, you should have a dime's worth of clearance at each hinge edge and in between. Usually, making one cut on the jointer and slightly easing the corners with sandpaper will produce the required clearance. If not, make a second cut on the jointer.

If the face frame has no bottom rail, you'll have to cut the doors and bottom drawer to length after jointing both edges and the top end. Place the drawer and doors in their openings, with the proper clearance all around. Lay a straightedge across them, aligned with the bottom ends of the stiles, and lightly mark for the cuts. Make the cuts using the cutoff box, then joint the bottom end.

Frame-and-Panel Faces

Frame-and-panel door and drawer faces add depth and richness to a kitchen. They are made of either a plywood or a solid-wood panel fitted into a solid-wood frame. A plywood panel may be glued into the frame, but a solid-wood panel must be free to move with changes in humidity.

Frames and panels can be used for any face: rabbeted for lip faces, beveled or left square for overlay faces and fit into the face-frame openings for flush faces. If a drawer is too small to use a frame-and-panel face, you can use the panel alone. Unlike the grain on plywood drawer faces, which runs vertically, the grain on frame-and-panel drawer panels should run horizontally. Door panels run vertically.

Though many designs for raised frame-and-panel faces require a spindle shaper, some simple ones can be made with just the tablesaw, jointer and router. I'll discuss the one shown below: a frame with a solid-wood raised panel.

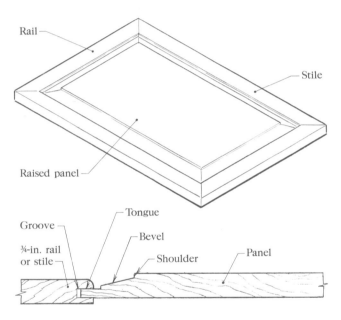

A solid-wood, frame-and-panel face can be made as a lip, overlay or flush face. The panel is free to move in the groove as it expands and contracts.

Making the frame—Begin with the frame, because it's easier to make the panel tongue fit the frame groove than vice versa.

1. The solid wood for the frame parts (the horizontals are rails and the verticals are stiles, just like on the face frame) should be free of knots, splits and twist. Select enough to make several extra pieces, in case some are ruined during machining. The pieces should all be planed to the same thickness (¾ in. will do). Rough-cut the pieces to lengths that are easy to handle, long enough to make one, two, or three frame parts with enough extra for trimming later.

2. Joint one edge of all the pieces straight and square to the face. (If the stock is wide enough to rip two parts, joint both edges.) Rip the rails and stiles ⅟₁₆ in. wider than finished width—always put the jointed edge against the rip fence. In one pass, joint the rough-cut edge of all the parts to final width.

3. Next, bullnose and groove the inside of the frame parts. Study the cuts to determine the order in which they can most effectively be made. Rout the bullnose first; if you machine the groove first, the pilot on the bit that cuts the bullnose might not have enough wood to support it. (These pieces are small, so it's safest to rout them using the shaper table.)

4. The ¼-in.-wide groove could also be routed, but bits that small can break easily. I suggest using the tablesaw, making several cuts with a carbide blade or one with a dado head. If you use a sawblade, make both outside cuts first and, if necessary, remove the remaining wood from the center with another cut. Make the grooves deep (½ in. or so) to allow for panel shrinkage. Use a feather board to hold the frame part firmly against the fence, as shown in the drawing below. Make the feather board from a piece of straight-grained hardwood, 6 in. to 8 in. wide. For easy clamping, make it long enough to extend from the blade to the edge of the saw table. Cut one end at a 60° angle and draw a line parallel to this end and about 8 in. from it. Rip a series of cuts from the angled end to the line to make fingers about ⅜ in. wide.

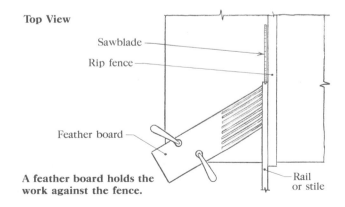

A feather board holds the work against the fence.

To position the feather board, make a partial cut in a rail or stile. With the machine turned off and the frame piece over the blade, clamp the board in place so that each of the fingers bends slightly, applying even pressure against the piece. When the groove and bullnose have been cut, sand the pieces.

5. Cut the joints next. The frame can be butt-jointed and doweled, like the face frame, but if it is, the groove must be cut blind and the bullnose routed after assembly. I prefer to do all machining before assembly and to hide end grain, so I use miter joints for these frame. Miter joints look nice and are fairly strong, even if they're only glued, though you can re-inforce them with long finish nails or splines. Mitered frames glued to plywood panels are very strong. (See p. 118 for how to make a cutoff box for mitering.) Whichever joint you choose, the door or drawer frame must be cut to fit into or overlap the face frame, depending on the style of face. When you've cut the joints, set the frame aside (don't assemble it) and make the panel.

Making the raised panel—Wood for solid-wood panels should be free of knots and splits, but knots don't matter as much in panels as in frames. The panel can be thinner than the frame or it can be the same thickness, so it will protrude beyond the frame.

1. Rough-cut the wood 1 in. to 2 in. more than the length of the panels. Remember that the grain of a door panel should run vertically; the grain of a drawer panel, horizontally. If the panel is wider than the available wood, you'll need to join several pieces together edge to edge. After the glue has dried, plane the panel to its finished thickness. Keep a couple of pieces of scrap of finished thickness for setting up the saw and router later on.

2. Joint one edge of each panel, then rip the panels to width on the tablesaw. To determine the width of each, lay out its frame and measure between the bottoms of the stile grooves. Make the panel at least ¼ in. narrower than this measurement. Wider panels should be even narrower—a 24-in.-wide panel may shrink (or expand) ⅜ in. or so across its width.

3. Trim one end square and cut the panel to length using the cutoff box. There is little movement with the direction of the grain, so the length need be only ⅛ in. less than the distance between the grooves.

4. Now you're ready to raise the panel. This is done with two cuts on the tablesaw. I cut the bevel first, then lay the panel face down and cut the shoulder. The angle and length of the bevel are variable, depending on your taste, but remember that the end of the bevel shouldn't be thinner than the width of the groove. (It will be routed to fit later.) Make a few test cuts on panel scraps to make sure that the setup is right. When making a bevel cut on slightly bowed panels, use the feather board to help keep them tight against the fence. Be sure to position the board in front of the sawblade so that it doesn't push the waste into the blade.

Make the shoulder cut next. It should intersect the bevel cut to leave a clean corner. Take care to use a push stick on the shoulder cut so the waste won't kick back. (The shoulder can be cut before the bevel if the throat plate in the saw will support the edge or end of the panel as it is being cut. That way, the waste won't be between the blade and the fence when it's cut loose.)

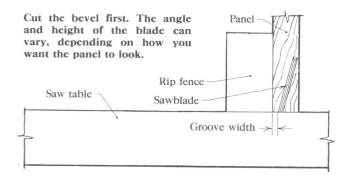

Cut the bevel first. The angle and height of the blade can vary, depending on how you want the panel to look.

Panel · Rip fence · Saw table · Sawblade · Groove width

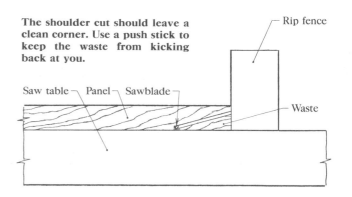

The shoulder cut should leave a clean corner. Use a push stick to keep the waste from kicking back at you.

Rip fence · Saw table · Panel · Sawblade · Waste

5. Use the router shaper table to make a tongue on the panel. Though the tongue should fit snugly in the frame groove, it shouldn't be too tight. Make the tongue long enough to allow for expected expansion. Check the setup using the scrap pieces you cut when setting up to raise the panel.

6. Sand the panel. You can sand the beveled surfaces by wrapping the paper around a wooden block cut to fit between the shoulder and the tongue.

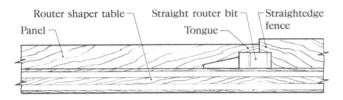

Cut the tongue using the router shaper table. The tongue should be a snug fit in the groove, but not too tight.

Assembly—It's often easier to assemble a frame-and-panel face after the parts have been finished: glue won't stick to most finishes, so there's less chance of gluing the panel to the frame. If the panel has no finish, be sure no glue touches it. Assemble the panels dry to make sure everything fits.

1. If you've doweled and butt-jointed your frames, use bar clamps during assembly. Glue two parts to a third, insert the panel and add the last part. Make sure the assembled face is lying on a flat surface when you clamp it—a twisted face is hard to correct. Measure across the diagonals to check that the frame is square. If not, adjust the clamps.

Mitered frames are harder to clamp—they tend to slide out of bar clamps. I use a clamping jig, as shown in the drawing below at left. Put pieces of paper under each joint so you don't glue the frame to the base. When the glue is applied, the miters will slide; tap the wedges into place carefully until the miters are tight and the inside corners even.

After the glue has cured, I add a spline to each corner, using the jig shown in the drawing below to kerf for the spline. Plane the spline to thickness—it should fit the kerf snugly. Glue the spline with its grain running at a right angle to the miter.

2. Drive a small brad through each rail into the panel back. Center the brads lengthwise, and the same amount of tongue will show at each stile when the panel shrinks.

3. Plane the faces of the frame flush with one another. The assembled frame-and-panel faces can now be treated like the other faces: fit over the opening for overlay faces, set in the opening for flush faces and rabbeted for lip faces.

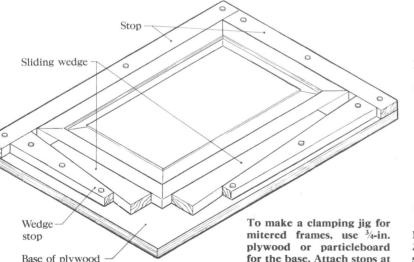

To make a clamping jig for mitered frames, use ¾-in. plywood or particleboard for the base. Attach stops at right angles to each other.

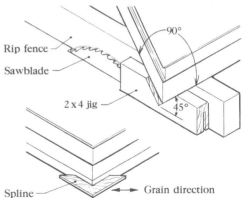

Make a kerfing jig for splined miters from a 2x4 or 2x6 that has been planed flat and square. Use a push stick to keep the frame and jig tight against the rip fence.

Drawer Construction

Chapter 10

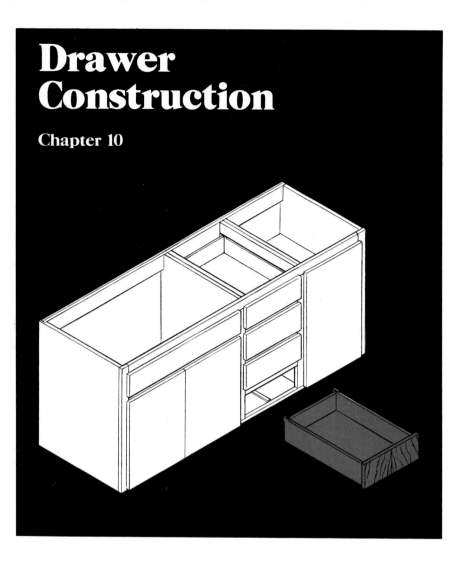

In this chapter, I'll describe how to make simple drawers and two systems of supporting and guiding the drawers in the cabinet. The support and guide systems affect a drawer's construction, so it's best to look at these systems first.

Several features are required of a good system. It should be strong enough to support a loaded drawer and guide it easily in and out of the cabinet. It should support the drawer by its sides, not the bottom; bottoms may warp or bow under loads, causing the drawer to shift vertically in the face frame or bind in the case. The system should also provide some means of adjusting the drawer's depth in the case, its horizontal position, and the amount the drawer drops when it is opened. Though you should

always strive for accuracy, it helps if the system is forgiving of slight errors in the case or drawer construction, without affecting looks or operation. Finally, a good system should be relatively easy to build and to operate.

Both systems discussed here are good ones. Either can be used with lip, overlay or flush faces and simple drawers. In the first system, which you can make yourself, a grooved wooden slide attached to the drawer bottom runs on a guide strip attached to the dust panel (as shown in the top drawing on the opposite page). This center-guide system is quite forgiving and is easy to adjust horizontally. The weight of the drawer is supported by its sides, which slide on the dust panel.

Commercially made metal slides make drawer construction a bit easier—you don't have to make slides and guides. But metal-slide systems can't be adjusted horizontally and aren't forgiving of errors. As shown in the bottom drawing below, half of each slide is attached to the drawer side, the other half to the case. The drawer is guided and supported by the slides.

Wooden Slides and Guides

If you choose the center-guide system, the wooden slides and guides should be made and the guides installed before the case is assembled. After assembly, it's difficult to work inside the case to attach the guides. The slides are made of ½-in. plywood (either hardwood or softwood), and the guides are made of a solid, straight-grained wood, such as fir, Alaskan cedar or walnut.

1. Make the slides first. Rough-cut the plywood approximately 1 in. longer than the total depth of the case, and approximately 2¼ in. wide. (The width isn't critical, but it should be the same for all the slides.)

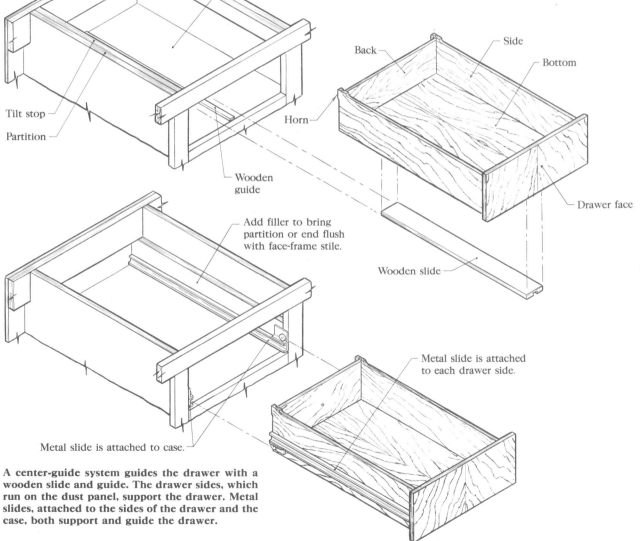

A center-guide system guides the drawer with a wooden slide and guide. The drawer sides, which run on the dust panel, support the drawer. Metal slides, attached to the sides of the drawer and the case, both support and guide the drawer.

The grain of the face veneer should run along the length of the pieces. Make at least one extra slide, in case one is ruined during machining later on.

2. Make the groove on the tablesaw, using a single sawblade or dado head set to cut through all but two veneers of the plywood. The groove should be slightly less than ¾ in. wide and should be centered on the piece. If you're using a single blade, set the rip fence so you can cut the sides of the groove by indexing each edge against the fence. Make these two cuts in all the slides without moving the fence. Keep the slide tight against the fence, because any slight error will affect the drawer's operation.

3. There are several ways to remove the remainder of the wood from the groove. If you're making only a few slides, make a series of saw cuts in the waste, then clean out any slivers in the groove with a chisel.

To make a lot of slides, set up the router with a ½-in. or ⅝-in. straight bit in the shaper table to clean out the waste. When routing, don't let the bit touch the sides of the groove—the bit could bend some of the wood fibers, which would then act like fingers, making the slide difficult to move on the guide.

4. Make the guide strips next. Use pieces of straight-grained wood wide enough to yield a number of strips. Plane these pieces as thick as the width of the grooves in the slides. (If a planer is unavailable, you can rip the thickness on a tablesaw.) The pieces should fit into the groove snugly, so that after they're cut into strips, a light cut with a hand plane will make a perfect sliding fit.

5. Joint both edges of the pieces, then rip a guide off each. Repeat until you've made enough. The thickness of the guides should be equal to or slightly less than the depth of the groove in the slides.

Installing the guides

1. It's much easier to attach the guide strips to the dust panels before assembling the case than it is to do it afterward. To position them, use the horizontal stick to mark the approximate center of the drawer opening on the dust panels. (Remember that the center of the opening may not be the center of the panel if a stile overlaps at one end of the panel but not the other. Within ½ in. is close enough.) Then make a mark half the width of the guide strip away from the center mark.

2. Use a gauge to position the guide strips. The gauge ensures that the guides are parallel to the ends of the dust panel and bottom, and its straight edge can be used to straighten any bowed guide strips. Make the gauge from ¼-in. or ½-in.-thick plywood scrap. Rip it as wide as the distance from the end of the dust panel to the mark indicating the edge of the guide strip (the second mark made in step 1). If the dust panels are dadoed into a finish or hidden end, make the gauge to index against those ends of the dust panels. This way, you can index against the corresponding end of the cabinet bottom (as shown in the drawing below), so that the guide strips on the dust panels and the bottom line up. If both ends of each dust panel are dadoed into partitions, you will have to use the horizontal story stick to locate the position of the guide on the cabinet bottom. Mark the position of the guide, tack the gauge at the mark, parallel to the end of the bottom, and position the guide against the gauge.

3. Trim one end of the guides and cut them to length (¹⁄₁₆ in. less than the width of the dust panel).

4. Tack the gauge flush to the end of the dust panel with a couple of box nails. Spread a light film of glue on the guide, position it tight against the gauge and a little shy of both edges of the dust panel. Nail it with ⅝-in. or ¾-in. brads. Move the gauge to the next dust panel and repeat this step.

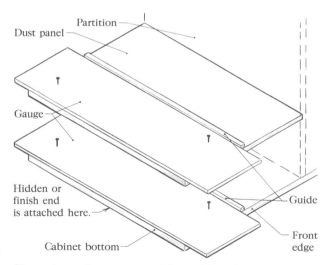

Use a plywood gauge to position guide strips.

Be sure to mark each of the dust panels so that they don't get turned around during assembly. The way in which the bottom will go into the case is usually obvious, but it doesn't hurt to mark that, too.

Tilt stops—When the face-frame rails between the drawers are wider than the thickness of the dust panels, you'll need to add tilt stops to the case to keep the drawers from tilting downward as they are pulled out. (If you're not using a face frame, the dust panels will prevent all the drawers, except the top one, from tilting. A drawer below a breadboard uses the breadboard track shown on p. 81 as a tilt stop.)

Make the tilt stops from waste plywood. They should be flush with the lower edge of the face-frame rail or up to ¹⁄₁₆ in. below it. Use one or several pieces to make the correct thickness. Cut them wide enough for the drawer side to bear on them, and as long as the width of the dust panel (or ¹⁄₁₆ in. less).

Before gluing the tilt stops to the dust panels, turn the case upside down. Gravity will help hold the tilt stops in place as the glue dries. (I rip the drawer sides to width now, as discussed in step 1 on p. 72, making them a snug fit, and use them to hold the tilt stops while the glue dries. This also ensures that the distance between the tilt stop and the dust panel below it will be equal on both sides of the drawer, which is necessary for the drawer to operate smoothly.)

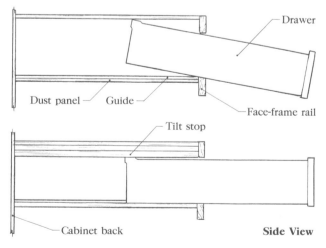

Tilt stops keep the drawer from tilting downward as it is pulled out.

Metal Slides

There are many metal-slide systems for drawers on the market. Most have to be fastened to the inside of the cabinet on a surface flush with the edge of a face-frame stile. When you can't place the cabinet end or partition flush with the stile, you'll need to install fillers, as shown in the drawing below. The fillers can be made of one or more thicknesses of plywood or solid wood. I prefer to fasten these fillers with several screws and no glue. Later, if the drawer turns out to be too narrow, you can compensate by using a thicker filler.

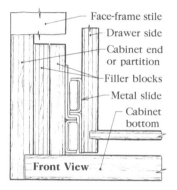

For metal slides, add filler blocks if the stile is not flush with an end or a partition.

Lip-Face Drawers

The simple drawer construction shown in the top drawing on p. 72 will work for all styles of faces and for center-guide and metal-slide systems, with just a few changes for each. I'll describe how to make lip-face drawers with center-guide systems and point out where the methods must be altered if you're using a metal-slide system.

The drawer sides and back are ½ in. thick and the bottom is ¼ in. thick. Fir plywood is commonly used for drawer sides, backs and bottoms in kitchen cabinets. You can also use solid wood, hardwood plywood or unidirectional plywood. (Unidirectional plywood is made with the grain of all the plies running in the same direction. Though it warps too much to be used in wide pieces, it makes nice drawer sides and backs.)

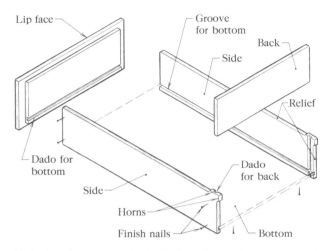

This drawing shows a basic lip-face drawer. The method of attaching the face to the sides varies for flush-face and overlay-face drawers.

The drawer faces have already been cut to size and rabbeted, as explained in Chapter 9. Now you must widen the rabbet on each edge of the face by ½ in. or more to take the drawer side, or the drawer side and metal slide, as shown in the drawing below. To do this, you can use the same setup for the router shaper table or the tablesaw that you used to make the rabbets for the lips.

For metal slides, the rabbet should be ¼ in. wider than the combined thickness of the drawer side and metal slide. The width of the drawer is critical when using metal slides. Be sure to follow the instructions that come with the slides you buy.

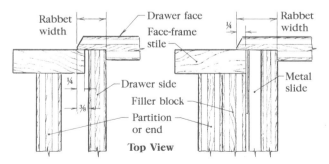

The width of the rabbets for drawer sides differs in the center-guide system (left) and metal-slide system (right).

Drawer sides

1. Rough-cut the wood for the drawer sides to length, about 1 in. longer than the depth of the cabinet. Then rip the drawer sides to final width: the distance between the face-frame rails that form the drawer opening, or the distance between the tilt stop or breadboard track and the dust panel. Make the sides fit the opening tightly—clearance will be routed later. (Metal slides require widths smaller than the opening; again, check the instructions.)

2. Trim one end and finish-cut the sides ¹⁄₃₂ in. to ¹⁄₁₆ in. longer than cabinet depth, measured from the face of the face frame to the back. (Metal slides usually require drawer sides shorter than cabinet depth.)

3. If the sides are bowed, put the convex face on the inside of the drawer. Look for blemishes on the plywood and place them where they are least likely to show. Then mark the outside face of each drawer side near or at its back bottom corner; the placement of this identification mark is the key to many of the following machining operations. Mark the dust panels and bottom with the numbers that correspond to the sides of the drawers that slide on them.

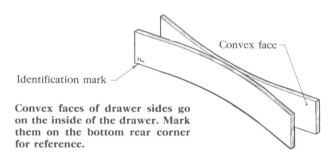

Convex faces of drawer sides go on the inside of the drawer. Mark them on the bottom rear corner for reference.

4. Cut the dadoes (grooves across the grain) in the sides to house the drawer back. Set up the router in the shaper table with a ½-in. straight bit. Adjust the fence and bit depth to cut a ¼-in.-deep dado for the drawer back about ½ in. in from the end. Dado all the drawer sides using the same setup. The identification mark should be on the face opposite the cut.

5. Each drawer side needs two horns at its upper rear corner: one on the top of the corner, one on the end. The top horns of a drawer bear against the dust panel or tilt stop to control the tilt of the drawer as it

is pulled out of the case; the end horns strike the back of the case to stop the drawer. Drawers with horns slide easier because there is less friction. Use the shaper table and a ½-in. straight bit to rout the reliefs that form the horns. The fence should have a ⅛-in. step to support the wood as it passes the bit.

Cut a relief along the back end, leaving about ¾ in. at the top. A back-up block will help to keep narrow drawer sides from twisting during the cut, as shown below. Cut another relief along the top edge, leaving about 1¼ in. at the back. Note where the identification mark is in relation to the horns.

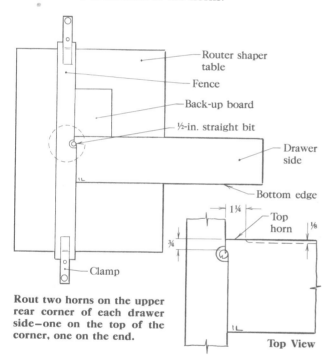

- Router shaper table
- Fence
- Back-up board
- ½-in. straight bit
- Drawer side
- Bottom edge
- Clamp

1¼

Top horn

⅛

¾

Top View

Rout two horns on the upper rear corner of each drawer side—one on the top of the corner, one on the end.

6. Now test all the drawer sides in their openings. If they fit too tightly, plane a bit off the top horn. The sides should slide easily, but not sloppily.

7. Rout the groove for the drawer bottom in each drawer side, using the router shaper table and a ¼-in. straight bit. The groove should be exactly the same depth as the dado for the drawer back. (Use one of these dadoes as a gauge for this setup.) Position the fence at a distance from the bit equal to the thickness of the drawer slide plus ¹⁄₁₆ in. This extra space will raise the slide above the dust panel so the slide only

guides the drawer and carries no weight. (The position of the drawer bottom isn't critical if you are using metal slides. Make it approximately ½ in. from the bottom edge.)

8. If the drawer faces have no lip on their bottom ends, use the same setup to rout the dado for the bottom in the drawer face. For drawer faces with a lip on their bottom ends, set the router fence ¹³⁄₁₆ in. from the bit to raise the rabbet ⅛ in. above the face-frame rail, as shown in the drawing below. (For drawers with metal slides, position the dado in the drawer face so the bottom edge of the drawer side will be suspended about ⅛ in. to ¼ in. above the dust panel. The lip should still overlap the frame ¼ in.)

9. Use the same setup to rout out the drawer face for the slide. Mark the area where the slide attaches, then place the dado you've routed in the face over the bit and move the face in and out between the marks until all the waste has been routed out. It's okay to rout freehand—the fence will keep you from cutting beyond the dado. Be sure that you make the space for the slide wider than the width of the slide, to allow for adjustment.

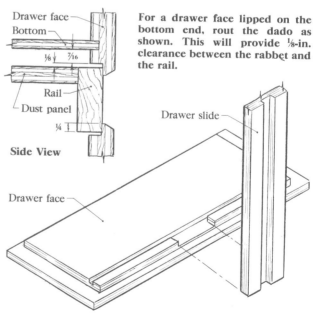

- Drawer face
- Bottom
- ⅛   ⁷⁄₁₆
- Rail
- Dust panel
- ¼

Side View

- Drawer slide
- Drawer face

For a drawer face lipped on the bottom end, rout the dado as shown. This will provide ⅛-in. clearance between the rabbet and the rail.

Rout the back of the drawer face to take the drawer slide. Make the area wider than the slide to allow for adjustment.

Drawer bottoms and backs

1. After the sides and faces have been machined, cut the drawer bottoms and backs. Find the width of the bottom and length of the back (they're the same) by holding the sides against the rabbets in the face and measuring between the grooves in the sides.

2. The length of the drawer bottom is ⅛ in. less than the length of the grooves in the drawer sides, measured from the front end of the side through the dado for the back. (The ⅛ in. is the difference between the depths of the dado and the rabbet in the drawer face.) The bottom should just cover the back.

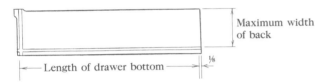

The length of the drawer bottom is ⅛ in. shorter than the length of the grooves in the side, measured through the dado for the back.

3. The drawer back sits on top of the drawer bottom. The width of the back is not really critical, but it shouldn't be any wider than the distance from the top of the groove to the relief on the top edge on the drawer side.

4. Rip all the drawer bottoms and backs to width, then trim and crosscut them to length using the cut-off box. The dimensions of the bottoms and the length of the backs will be the same for all the drawers in a stack, though there may be some difference in the width of the backs.

5. Check to make sure the bottoms fit their grooves and the backs fit their dadoes. If the bottoms or backs are too thick, you can cut a slight rabbet with a router or tablesaw to make them fit (p. 41).

6. Sand all the drawer parts before assembly. Sand the outside of the drawer faces by hand or with a straight-line sander. Hand-sand the edges and ends of drawer faces and lightly ease the corners. The faces of the other parts may be sanded with the orbital sander. Hand-sand the top edges of the drawer sides and backs.

Assembly—Collect all the materials you will need for assembly before you start: hammer, nail set, framing square, glue, rags, short bar clamp, hand-screw clamp, 3d finish nails, ⅝-in. or ¾-in. brads, and a small scrap of ¼-in. plywood. Polyvinyl or aliphatic glue sets quickly, so assembly should progress smoothly, without hesitation. Read through the following assembly steps before beginning to work.

1. Clamp the drawer face to the corner of the bench, rabbeted face up, and spread glue in its dado and rabbets. Then spread glue in the dado and grooves of the sides. Be sure there is a film of glue on every contact surface of each joint.

2. Put the drawer bottom and one side in place and nail the side to the face with two or three 3d finish nails. (It may be necessary to pull the end of the drawer side tight to the rabbet with a bar clamp while nailing.)

3. Rotate the face 90° on the bench for easy clamping and nailing, and nail the second side in place.

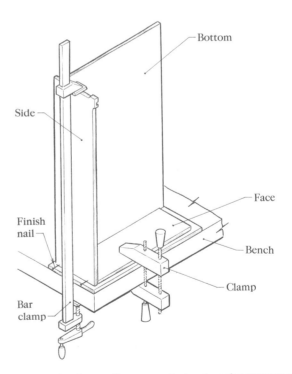

Clamp the drawer face securely to a bench corner to assemble the bottom and first side. Then turn the drawer face 90° so you can nail and clamp on the other side. Pull the side tightly to the rabbet with a bar clamp while nailing.

4. Put glue on the bottom edge of the back, slide it into the dadoes in the sides and nail through the sides with 3d finish nails.

5. Invert the drawer and check its squareness with a framing square. If it is more than $\frac{1}{16}$ in. off, tap a back corner to square it up. (Drawers with metal slides must be very close to square or the drawer face won't close against the face frame on both edges.) Nail through the bottom into the face and back. Support the back with a piece of plywood scrap while nailing. Assemble all the drawers in the same way.

Installing the slides

1. Trim and cut the drawer slides to length. They shouldn't extend beyond the drawer back. Measure the position of a guide strip between the face-frame stiles; use this measurement to position the slide on the drawer bottom. Tack the slide at a right angle to the drawer face with a $\frac{5}{8}$-in. brad at each end.

Try the drawer in the case. When you look down at the drawer face from above, it should be parallel to the face of the face frame. The drawer should also be centered in the opening. If it doesn't fit as it should, remove it and tap the slide slightly from one side to the other as needed. When the first drawer has been adjusted, measure the distance between the slide and the drawer side. If the guides were installed using the same gauge and the machining was done as directed, this measurement can be used to install all the slides in the stack.

2. When you've installed the slides on all the drawers in a stack, put them in the case. Their faces should line up vertically, but if they don't, you can make final adjustments by tapping the slides one way or the other.

3. When all the drawers are adjusted, fasten the slides with two 3d finish nails at each end. Don't use glue because the slide may need adjustment later.

4. The end horns on the drawer sides should hit the cabinet back and stop the drawer when the lip is $\frac{1}{32}$ in. from the outside of the face frame. If the gap is greater than that amount, plane a little off each horn.

5. Rub a little paraffin on the top horns, on the bottom edges of the drawer sides and in the drawer slide. If the drawer sides still seem tight, plane a little off their top horns. The drawer should not tilt more than $\frac{1}{8}$ in. as it opens.

Flush-Face Drawers

I make flush-face drawers using a dovetail tenon and groove to attach the drawer side to the face. The dovetail tenon is routed along the width of the side; it slides into a dovetail groove routed in the drawer face. Dovetail tenons and grooves are stronger than the rabbets on lip-face drawers, but require greater skill to make. They work equally well for flush faces between face-frame rails or flush faces that overlap dust panels, as shown in the bottom drawing below.

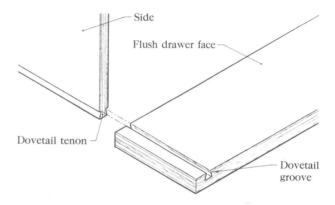

The sides and face of a flush-face drawer can be joined with a single dovetail tenon and dovetail groove.

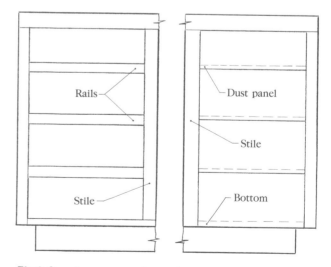

Flush-face drawers can be set between rails (left), or they can overlap the dust panels and bottom (right).

Drawer sides

1. Rough-cut ½-in.-thick stock for the sides. Make the sides about ½ in. longer than the distance from the front of the face frame to the cabinet back, and wide enough to fit their opening snugly. Save some of the scrap for the test cuts you'll need to make when setting up to cut the joints.

2. Trim and cut the drawer sides to final length: ⅜ in. longer than the width of the dust panel. (Sides for drawers with metal slides should be only ⅛ in. longer than the width of the dust panel.)

3. Arrange any sides that are warped so that the convex faces are on the inside of the drawer, and mark the sides.

4. Rout the dovetail groove in the face using the router shaper table. Chuck a ½-in. dovetail bit in the router and set it about 5/16 in. above the shaper table. Test the cut on the back end of a drawer side (the cut won't matter at the back). Place the drawer side in the case with the test cut next to the face frame. The shoulder of the cut should be between 1/32 in. and 1/16 in. in front of the back of the face frame; later, the end horn will be planed to allow the drawer face to fit flush with the cabinet face. Adjust the height of the bit if necessary.

The dovetail grooves should be about ½ in. from each edge of the drawer face. Position them by clamping a straightedge ½ in. from the bit. (Metal slides have to be positioned accurately on this setup; the width of the assembled drawer must be less than the width of the opening by a given amount—be sure to check the instructions.) Holding the drawer face tightly against the table and against the fence, rout the dovetail grooves.

5. Next, machine the dovetail tenons on the ends of the drawer sides. Without changing the height of the bit from the previous setup, move the straightedge to cover most of the bit, as shown in the drawing below. Make a test cut in a scrap of drawer-side material. (This test piece must be exactly the same thickness as the drawer sides.) Rout across both faces of one end, then try the tenon in the drawer-face groove. The parts should slide together quite easily (when the glue is applied, the wood will swell and the joint will be harder to assemble), but a joint that is too loose won't be very strong. The gap between the dovetail shoulder and the drawer face should be no more than 1/16 in. When the setup is correct, rout the front end of each drawer side. (Remember that the identification mark is on the back end.)

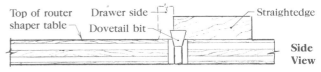

Set up the fence to rout the dovetail tenons as shown, without changing the height at which the bit was set for routing the dovetail grooves.

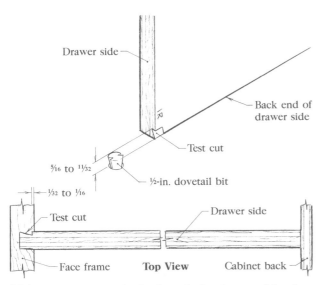

Make a test cut on the back end of a drawer side, then check it inside the case. The shoulder of the cut should fall on the face frame, as shown.

6. Before dismantling the setup, test-fit all the tenons. A tenon may not fit if the drawer sides vary in thickness or if sawdust has kept one away from the shaper-table fence. Rout these tenons again using the same setup. If a tenon still doesn't fit, move the fence slightly to remove a little more wood.

7. The rest of the drawer, including bottoms and backs, is made as described previously for a lip-face drawer, except for two differences in the machining operations. The first is to leave a top horn at both

the front and back ends of the drawer side, otherwise an unsightly, empty dovetail groove will show.

8. The second operation involves a different way of cutting the dado for the bottom in the drawer face. (For a flush drawer face that fits between face-frame rails, use the setup that you used to rout the grooves in the sides.) For a drawer face that covers the dust panel on which it slides, as shown in the drawing on p. 75, you must reset the fence on the shaper table after routing the grooves in the sides. To find the position of the dado in the face, slide the bottom in the drawer sides and place the partially assembled drawer in the case. Measure from the bottom of the dust panel above this drawer to the drawer bottom. This is how far the dado should be from the top end of the drawer face. If the measurement differs from side to side, average them. Set the fence at this measurement from the bit. Cut a piece of scrap, 4 in. to 5 in. wide and as long as or longer than the drawer face, and rout a dado along its width, pushing one end against the fence. Slide the dado on the bottom of the partially assembled drawer in the case. The gap between the top end of the scrap and the bottom of the dust panel should be no more than $\frac{1}{32}$ in.

When the setup is correct, rout the drawer face between the dovetail grooves only, indexing the top end against the fence. Repeat this procedure for all the drawers in a stack. Then rout out on the back of the face for the wooden slide, as described on p. 73.

9. For clearance, joint a bevel of approximately 5° on the top and bottom ends of the drawer face.

Assembly—Sand the face and the other parts, then assemble the drawers dry and try them in the case. If the side clearances for the metal slides and the face clearances are okay, collect all the materials you'll need before you continue: hammer, nail set, framing square, polyvinyl or aliphatic glue, short bar clamp, hand-screw clamp, 3d finish nails, ⅝-in. or ¾-in brads and a small scrap of ¼-in. plywood.

1. Clamp the face to the corner of the bench. Apply glue to the bottom dado and dovetail grooves in the face and to the grooves and dovetail tenons of the sides. Slide the drawer sides into place, and wipe up the glue that is pushed out of the dovetail grooves. Then slide the drawer bottom into place. This locks the drawer sides perpendicular to the face.

2. Try the partially assembled drawer in the case. If you find the drawer face is too high or low in relationship to the dust panel above, tap the face up or down on the drawer sides. The clearance shouldn't be much greater than $\frac{1}{32}$ in.

3. When the position is correct, clamp the face to the bench, clamp one side to the face, and toenail through the side into the face. Rotate the face 90° and clamp and nail the second side to the face. Remove the clamps, add the back and complete the assembly in the same manner as for a lip-face drawer. Try the drawer in the case again immediately. Slight vertical adjustments can be made with light taps of a hammer before the glue sets. When all the drawers are assembled, cut and attach the slides (p. 75).

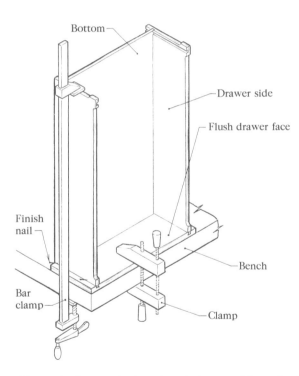

Clamp the face to the bench and clamp a side to the face. Then toenail through the side into the face.

Overlay-Face Drawers

Overlay-face drawers can be made using dovetail tenons and grooves, but the groove will show even when the drawer is closed unless you make it blind. Blind dovetail grooves are cut using the same technique you would use to cut a blind dado (p. 41).

Overlay drawers can also be made with false fronts and attached faces, as shown in the drawing below. This method of making drawers can be used with lip faces and flush faces, too. It reduces machining and handling of the face material, though it requires a little more material and slightly reduces the space in the drawer. This is the type of overlay-face drawer I'll discuss here.

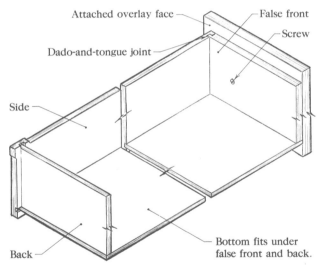

Attached overlay face — False front
— Screw
Dado-and-tongue joint
Side
Back — Bottom fits under false front and back.

Drawers with false fronts can be used with any style of face. This drawing shows an overlay face that has been screwed on.

An overlay drawer with a false front is made exactly like the lip-face drawer discussed on pp. 71-75, except that the false front is joined to the sides with a dado-and-tongue joint. Make the false front of the same material as the sides. You've already cut the faces to size, so follow the steps on p. 72 to prepare and joint the drawer sides. Then cut a narrow dado in each drawer side.

1. Set a sawblade that cuts a ⅛-in. to ³⁄₁₆-in. kerf to cut this dado the same depth as the groove for the bottom in a drawer side. Adjust the rip fence so that the distance from the outside of the blade to the fence is ¹⁄₆₄ in. more than the thickness of the false front. (This will place the false front slightly behind the end of the drawer side and make a tight fit between the side and the overlay face.) Kerf the inside of the front end of each drawer side, as shown in the drawing below.

2. The width of false fronts and backs can be determined from the drawer sides. The width of the drawer bottoms (which is the distance between the sides plus the depth of the side grooves) determines the outside dimension of the drawer. There should be a ⅛-in. to ¼-in. clearance between each side and the opening, so be sure that you rip the drawer bottoms accordingly.

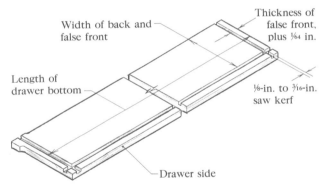

Width of back and false front
Thickness of false front, plus ¹⁄₆₄ in.
Length of drawer bottom
⅛-in. to ³⁄₁₆-in. saw kerf
Drawer side

Kerf each drawer side to take the tongue on the false front.

(Metal slides require an exact drawer width in relation to the frame opening. For many metal slides, the clearance needed is ½ in. on each side. Check the instructions for your slides.)

3. If care was taken to make the dadoes and grooves in the drawer sides the same depth, the false fronts and backs are as long as the bottom is wide. Set up the cutoff box with a stop block to cut the backs and false fronts to that length.

Here's an easy way to use the cutoff box to make one piece exactly as long as another—in this case, a drawer back as long as the width of the drawer bottom. Clamp a stop block to the push bar about 4 in. farther from the sawblade than the width of the drawer bottom. Place the bottom against the stop and a scrap piece against the bottom, as shown in the drawing below, then cut the scrap. Now put the scrap against the stop, put the trimmed end of the drawer back against the scrap and cut it to length (which will be exactly the same as the bottom).

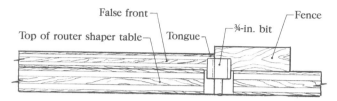

Rout the tongues on the false front. They should fit snugly in the kerf-cut dadoes in the drawer sides.

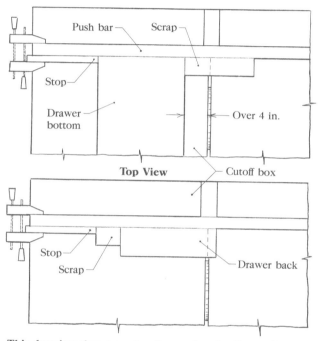

This drawing shows a setup for cutting duplicate pieces.

6. Spread an even film of glue in all the dadoes and grooves, and assemble the parts—bottom, sides, back and false front. Nail through the sides into the false front and the back with 3d finish nails.

7. Turn the drawer upside down and check it with a framing square. If the drawer is out of square by more than 1/16 in., tap one of its back corners to square it up. (Drawers with a center-guide system are somewhat forgiving, and can be out of square by the amount of the side clearance and still work. Metal slides, however, require a square drawer.) Then nail the bottom to the false front and back with 2d or 3d box nails.

8. When all the drawers are assembled, attach the drawer faces to the false fronts with screws driven from inside the drawer. Use several gauge blocks to help ensure a uniform lap on the face-frame rails, as shown in the drawing below. Drawer faces should overlap the stiles by the same amount as the door faces, which depends on the hinges used—many hinges require a 3/8-in. overlap. Attach the drawer slides as discussed on p. 75.

4. Drill 3/16-in. clearance holes in the false front for the No. 8 screws that will be used to attach it to the drawer face. Place a hole on each end (two on each end of false fronts over 3 in. wide). If the holes are too close to the edge or end, it will be hard to turn the screwdriver, but keep them as close as possible.

5. Rabbet each end of the false front to make the tongue. Set up the router in the shaper table as shown in the drawing above at right. The tongue should fit the dado easily, but snugly. Test the setup on scrap that is the same thickness as the false front. Sand the parts before assembly.

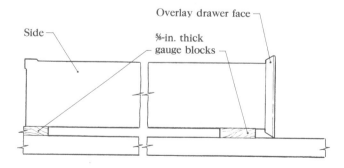

Use several gauge blocks to position the overlay face on the false front so it will overlap the face-frame rails correctly.

Breadboards

It might be said that no kitchen is complete without at least one breadboard. Breadboards provide added work or counter space, and a place to cut without fear of damage to expensive counter material. When a breadboard becomes damaged, it's easy to replace.

I like to slot a breadboard into the top rail of the face frame, because it is out of the way when not in use. The board runs on tracks that can be made from scraps—¾-in. plywood for the rails and solid wood for the guides. If you do this, the top rail of the face frame must be at least 2½ in. wide. When placing the breadboard, consider the completed design of the kitchen and the uses to which it will be put.

Record the placement of the breadboard when laying out the horizontal and vertical story sticks (p. 16).

The board—Edge-glued solid wood or birch plywood works quite well for the breadboard—avoid warped solid wood, though. With either material, the outside end should be capped with solid wood of the same species as the face frame. If both ends of the breadboard are capped, its life can be doubled by turning it over and around when one side becomes badly cut up.

1. For a solid-wood board, joint the edges of the pieces and glue them edge to edge. When the glue has set, plane the blank ¾ in. thick. Plane the material for the end caps ⅟₆₄ in. to ⅟₃₂ in. thicker than the board blank, and joint one edge.

2. Joint one edge of the breadboard blank straight and rip the blank to width: the opening in the face frame, less ⅛ in.

3. The completed breadboard (including end caps) should protude 1 in. beyond the face frame for flush and lip faces, and 1½ in. to 1¾ in. beyond the face frame for an overlay face. Rip the end caps 1½ in. to 2 in. wide, trim one end of the board blank, and cut it to length: the final length of the breadboard less the width of the two end caps.

4. Glue the end caps in place, jointed edge out. If you're using a solid-wood board, strengthen the joint with three or four dowels, but be careful not to put them where the finger-pull groove would intersect the dowel hole. Then clean up the joints with a hand plane and sandpaper. Use the cutoff box to trim the ends off the caps.

5. To rout finger-pull grooves in the end caps, chuck a ¾-in. corebox bit in the router and set up the shaper table, as shown in the drawing below. Mark the bit position on the face of the straightedge fence.

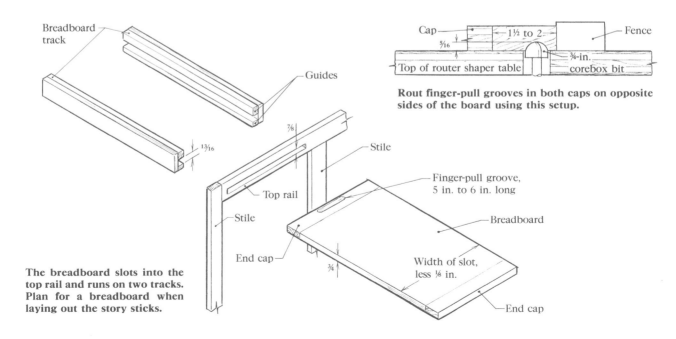

Rout finger-pull grooves in both caps on opposite sides of the board using this setup.

The breadboard slots into the top rail and runs on two tracks. Plan for a breadboard when laying out the story sticks.

Plan to rout a 5-in. or 6-in.-long finger-pull groove in each end and on opposite faces, but be sure to mark on the face opposite the groove. That way, you will know where to drop the board on the bit and when to lift it off.

The track – Two tracks are made on one piece of plywood and then ripped to exact width. Each track will be as wide as the top rail, and as long as the distance between the top rail and the nail rail. Some close-tolerance machining is required to avoid drag and wear in the wrong places, so take care when making the tracks.

1. Rough-cut a piece of ¾-in. plywood wider than two tracks and about 1 in. longer than needed.

2. Make the guides from solid wood about ¾ in. thick. Joint an edge straight and rip off four pieces ⅟₃₂ in. wider than the top portion of the face frame above the breadboard.

3. Glue and nail two of these guides flush with the two edges of the plywood-track blank, as shown in the drawing below. Rip a spacer from scrap about ⅟₁₆ in. thinner than the slot in the face frame, which is ⅛ in. wider than the breadboard thickness. Place the spacer next to each guide and glue and nail the other guides in place.

4. When the glue is dry, rip the tracks to the width of the face frame's top rail. If they are to act as a tilt stop, measure from the top of the top horn on the drawer side to the top of the rail, and rip them to that width. Cut the tracks to length. They should fit snugly between the top rail and the nail rail.

5. Slip the breadboard into the slot, put the tracks in place, tight against the board's edges, and put the drawer sides under them. Leave a ⅟₁₆-in. clearance between the breadboard and the ends of the slot in the top rail. (You may want to add filler blocks, as shown in the drawing below.) Glue, clamp and nail the track into the case. Leave the board between the track as a spacer until the tracks are fastened.

6. Rip or joint the board ⅟₁₆ in. narrower, so it can run easily between the tracks. If using the jointer, joint in 1 in. or so from an end, then turn the board around and joint from the other end, so you won't tear the end grain of the cap at the end of the cut.

7. Sand the faces and edges and dull all the corners. You can finish the end caps to match the cabinet, but use a nontoxic finish on the board's cutting surfaces. (Mineral oil is nontoxic and won't turn rancid like some vegetable oils.) Rub it in well and wipe off the excess. Oil the surface occasionally so it can be wiped clean easily.

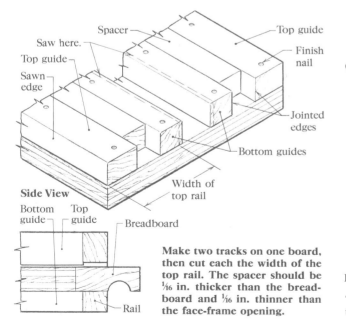

Make two tracks on one board, then cut each the width of the top rail. The spacer should be ⅟₁₆ in. thicker than the breadboard and ⅟₁₆ in. thinner than the face-frame opening.

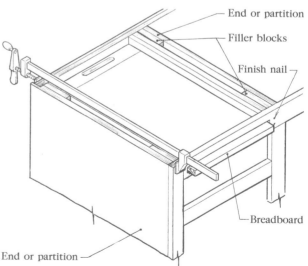

The tracks for the breadboard are glued and nailed into the case.

Installing Cabinet Hardware

Chapter 11

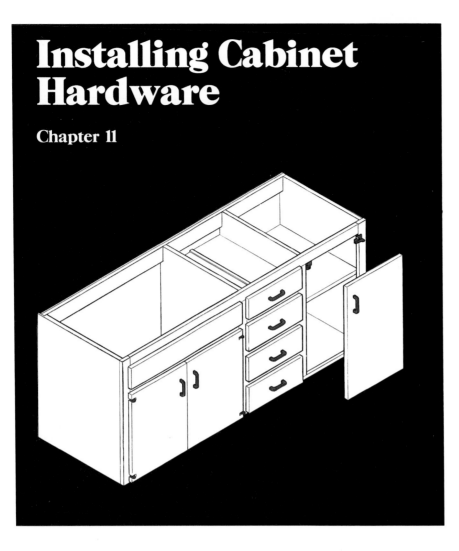

With the basic case assembled and the doors and drawers made, it's time to hinge and hang the doors and attach the pulls and catches. In addition to hinges, door pulls and catches, cabinets often require drawer slides (p. 69), shelf standard (p. 47), and specialty hardware (such as lazy Susans, spice racks and towel bars). Specialty hardware is so varied that it is impossible to describe its installation in generalities—you will have to follow the instructions that come with each item.

Hinges and pulls come in a variety of styles and colors to complement the decor of any kitchen. Some hinges are very ornate and show a great deal of metal; others are semiconcealed or completely hidden. There are hinges with springs that close the door automatically and hold it shut, eliminating the need for a catch. Some hinges can be adjusted, which is helpful when hanging flush-face doors.

The important factor in selecting hinges is that the hinges you choose must suit the particular face style that you are using. For example, a hinge made for a lip-face door will not work on a flush-face or on an overlay-face door.

When attaching hinges (and other hardware), it is very important that the pilot holes be centered in the slots or screw holes in the hinge flanges. Pilot holes that are drilled off center will cause the screw to pull the hinge out of alignment. (A self-centering bit will make centering pilot holes much easier, and is a worthwhile investment.)

Lip-Face and Beveled Overlay Doors

Most lip-face hinges have a door flange (one that fastens to the back of the door) and a stile flange (one that fastens to the stile of the face frame). These flanges are stepped to fit the ⅜-in. by ⅜-in. rabbet that forms the lip. (This is a standard dimension for lip-face hinges, but check to make sure before buying.) The hinge for beveled overlay doors is similar to the lip-face hinge, but the door flange isn't stepped down below the stile flange because the door rests on the surface of the face frame. The door flange is bent to accommodate the 60° bevel on the edge of the door.

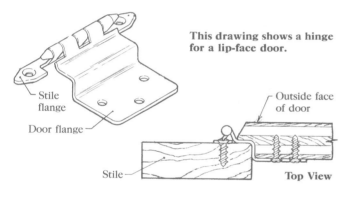

This drawing shows a hinge for a lip-face door.

Stile flange

Door flange

Stile

Outside face of door

Stile

Top View

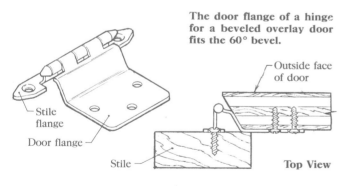

The door flange of a hinge for a beveled overlay door fits the 60° bevel.

Stile flange

Door flange

Stile

Outside face of door

Stile

Top View

Installing the hinges

1. Begin by laying the cabinet on its back. Put the doors, drawers and sink-apron face on the face frame, and align them correctly. (Edges of the doors under a sink apron, for example, should align with the edges of the sink-apron face.)

2. Remove a door, noting the edge to be hinged. Place its good face on a clean piece of carpet on the benchtop to avoid scratching. Now position the hinges. Many cabinetmakers use a hinge as a spacer, positioning all the hinges the length of one flange in from the door ends. (Whatever the distance from the ends, it should be the same for all the doors.)

3. Drill the pilot holes in the door back, using each hinge as a template to locate a self-centering bit. (The pilot hole's diameter should be about the same as the root diameter of the screw—the root is the solid center of the threaded portion of the screw.) Push each hinge against the surfaces of the rabbet and the door back on lip-face doors, and against the bevel and back on beveled overlay doors. Screw on the hinges.

4. Place the door on the case. It should be centered in its opening and line up with the other doors on the cabinet. Clamp a straightedge across the top or bottom of the face frame and push the end of each door against it to align them vertically.

Center the door horizontally, making sure the spaces between it and neighboring doors or drawers are even. Lip-face doors can be centered by feel and by eye. Beveled overlay doors, because of their overlap on the face frame, aren't as easy to center by eye. Use the gauge shown below to space them evenly.

When the door is positioned, drill pilot holes for the hinge in the stile, using the stile flange as a template. Screw the hinge to the stile. Repeat steps 2, 3 and 4 for each door on the cabinet.

The hinges shown in the drawing at left are also made with a spring so that they're self-closing. When installing this hinge, the spring will hold the stile flange at a slight angle to the face frame.

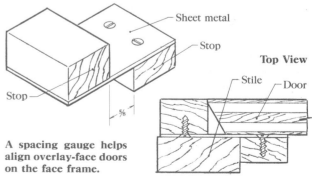

Sheet metal

Stop

Stop

Stop

⅝

Top View

Stile

Door

A spacing gauge helps align overlay-face doors on the face frame.

When the screws are drawn tightly to the flange of a self-closing hinge, the door will shift slightly away from the stile. When drilling the pilot holes, compensate for this movement by holding the door closer to the stile, or by pressing the flange down on the stile.

Flush-Face Doors

I hang flush-face doors on concealed hinges that allow only a bit of the hinge to show on the face of the door. These hinges are adjustable, so they are forgiving of small errors in alignment. Because they are designed specifically for overlay-face doors, however, cabinets with flush faces must be altered slightly if you are going to use this type of hinge. Several of the needed alterations must be made before the case is assembled. (Flush-face doors can be hung on butt hinges, but I don't recommend doing this for two reasons. First, butt hinges have to be screwed to the door edge, which does not hold screws well unless it's banded. Second, butt hinges aren't adjustable, so any errors cannot be corrected.)

Case alterations—The drawing below shows how flush-face doors can be hung using this type of concealed hinge. Doors at the hidden and finish ends (A) must be hinged on an inner stile in order to be flush with the face-frame stile. You can add an inner stile behind an intermediate face-frame stile on one or both sides of a partition (B). One or two doors can be hinged to the edge of a partition as in C and D. (The partition will be the same width as the hidden end and bottom. The banding covers the plies and anchors the hinge screws.) An inner stile attached to a partition as shown at E is an alternative to D. (The partition must be narrower than the hidden end by the thickness of the inner stile. Cut the partition to width using the tablesaw setup for the hidden end and bottom, but place the inner stile next to the fence when ripping.)

Doors can also be hung on an inner stile that isn't supported by a partition—imagine method E without the partition. The inner stile must be strong, so cut notches for it in any fixed shelves and the cabinet bottom. During case assembly, glue and nail this stile to the notches before attaching the face frame.

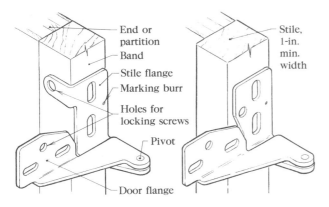

These concealed hinges can also be used to hang flush-face doors. Only the pivot shows on the face of the door.

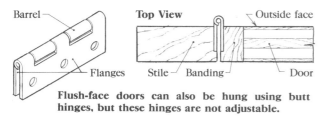

Flush-face doors can also be hung using butt hinges, but these hinges are not adjustable.

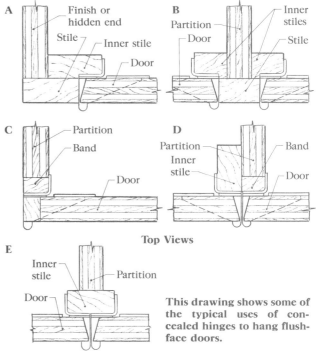

This drawing shows some of the typical uses of concealed hinges to hang flush-face doors.

Alterations to the case required by methods C, D and E must be made before the case is assembled. The inner stiles shown at A and B can be installed when the case is assembled or later on.

No matter which of these methods is used, you must allow for the hinge flanges, or the door won't be flush with the face frame. I do this by rabbeting the inner stiles as shown in A and B, and stop-jointing the partitions and inner stiles in C, D and E, as shown in the drawing below.

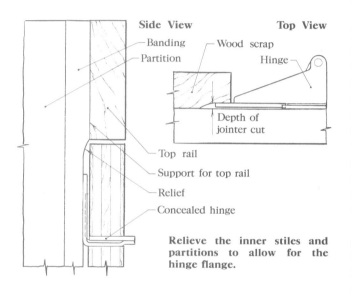

Relieve the inner stiles and partitions to allow for the hinge flange.

To cut the rabbet on the jointer, set the depth of cut to the depth of the rabbet, and set the fence for the width of the rabbet, as shown in the drawing below. (The width of the rabbet equals the width of the hinge's stile flange.) Joint the rabbet in one pass. You

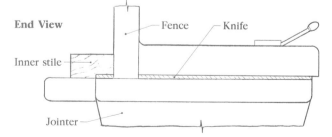

Set up the jointer as shown to cut a rabbet for the hinge.

are removing quite a bit of wood on a narrow piece, so be careful and use a push block. (You could also cut this rabbet on the tablesaw.)

The relief on a partition or intermediate inner stile is stop-jointed so there is wood left at the top end to support the face-frame rail. Move the jointer fence so the blade will cut across the full width of the edge (C, D) or face (E). Set a stop on the outfeed end of the jointer fence, or make a mark on the piece and joint to it. Be sure the nails in the partition banding are set beneath the depth of the cut. Go slowly at the end of the cut to leave a smooth surface where it stops.

Kerfing for the hinges—Each hinge fits in a slot cut in the edge of the door; its door flange is screwed to the back of the door. You've already cut the doors to fit the face-frame openings (p. 64), so the next step is to make the slots. You can cut this slot with a back-saw, but I recommend using the cutoff box, set up as shown in the drawing on p. 86. The sawblade's kerf will clear the waste in the slots. This setup makes it easy to kerf several doors quickly and accurately. Some blades will tear the underside of the door more than others will, so experiment on some scrap to find the best blade.

1. The door rests on the push bar of the cutoff box and against a straightedge nailed to the cutoff-box base. Position the straightedge using the door and a hinge, as shown in the drawing, so that the angled edge of the hinge's door flange is parallel to the cutoff-box base. The straightedge must also be parallel to the push bar. Nail the straightedge to the base, then saw through the straightedge.

2. Setting the height of the sawblade can be a little tricky because the slot angles into the edge and faces of the door. Make test cuts in a piece of scrap that is the same thickness as the door. Adjust the blade height until the end of the hinge's door flange comes flush with the edge of the door. (For most hinges of this type, the kerf will extend about $\frac{7}{16}$ in. from the edge on the face side of the door.)

3. Next, from the kerf in the straightedge, measure the distance of the hinges from the ends of the door (usually 1¼ in. to 1½ in.), and make a mark on the straightedge. Make another mark the same distance from the kerf on the other side. The ends of the doors are positioned against these marks for kerfing.

4. It will probably take more than one pass over the sawblade to make the slot wide enough for the hinge. Place the end of the scrap on one of the marks you've just made and cut a kerf. Move the scrap slightly and cut again to widen the slot. When the slot is wide enough, mark on the straightedge the position of the end of the scrap, so that you can position the door easily for the second kerf. Do the same on the other side.

5. When the setup is right, you're ready to kerf all the doors.

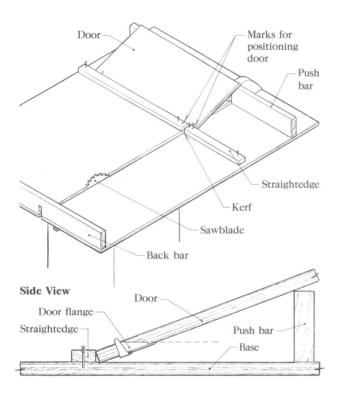

Side View

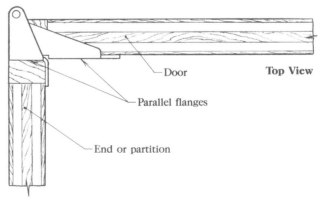

Use the cutoff box to kerf the door for concealed hinges. Place the straightedge so that the top edge of the flange on the door is parallel with the base.

Installing the hinges

1. Lay the case on its back on a flat bench. The slightest twist in the case will affect the fit of the doors. Sand the corners of the doors lightly and put all doors and drawers in place. The doors should clear the face frame by a dime's thickness on each edge and end. You'll have to find some way of keeping the doors from falling into the cabinet—catch mounts (p. 88) will help, if you've attached them.

2. Remove one door and place it face down on the carpet on the benchtop, with the hinge edge overhanging the bench slightly. Put the hinges in the slots. Be sure the ends of the door flanges are flush with the door edge, and the flange edge is tight against one side of the kerf to prevent the hinge from twisting. Use a self-centering bit to drill pilot holes in the center of the elongated slots, but not in the round locking holes. Attach each hinge to the door with just one screw, so it will be easy to remove later.

3. Carefully place the door on the case. It is extremely important that the door flange and the stile flange are parallel, as shown in the drawing below. Check that the clearance between the door and its neighbors is correct, then press on the door over the hinge, so the burr on the stile flange will mark the inner stile or the partition.

4. Remove the door from the case and the hinges from the door. Locate the indentation on the stile (or partition) and place the stile flange so the burr rests in it. Align the edges of the stile flange parallel with the edges of the stile or faces of the partition. If

When positioning the door and hinge on the case, make sure that the two flanges are parallel.

there's a locking tab on the stile flange, it should lay flat against the edge of the inner stile or the face of the partition. If necessary, shift the hinge horizontally until the tab is flush and the edges parallel. Be careful not to move it vertically—that would shift the position of the door in the opening, and the hinge might not align with the slot in the door.

5. When the stile flange is positioned, drill pilot holes through the center of its slots, and attach it to the inner stile or partition with screws in the slots only. Attach both hinges.

6. Open the hinges and attach the door with screws in the slots only. Adjust the clearance of the door by loosening the screws in the appropriate flange and tapping the door. When the clearance is uniform, tighten the screws.

When all the doors are in place, raise one corner of the case and notice how the clearances become uneven and the doors bind. Once you've installed the locking screws, you can't adjust the doors to compensate for this kind of racking. You can install the locking screws now while the case is flat on the bench, or later. If you add them now, make sure as you install the case that the toeboard is level and the case is scribed to the wall so the doors hang flush with the face frame and have uniform clearance all around. Don't fasten the case to the wall until you've checked these points.

If you decide to add the locking screws after installing the case, and the case racks out of square, you can plane and adjust the doors before putting in the screws. Planing will increase the clearance at the top or bottom of the door.

Door and Drawer Pulls

With the cabinet on its back, and the doors and drawers in place, set pulls on several doors and drawers. Door pulls should be placed near the door edge that isn't hinged: on lower cabinets, they should be near the top end of the door; on upper cabinets, near the bottom end. Drawer pulls are usually centered horizontally on the faces and, on the top-drawer faces, on or slightly above vertical center. All the other pulls should be the same distance from the top end of the drawer faces.

Once you are satisfied with the placement of the pulls, it is easy to install them, using two simple jigs I'll describe here.

The door-pull jig— Make the jig from ¾-in. scrap plywood, as shown in the drawing below. Lay out the position of the ³⁄₁₆-in. bolt holes for the pulls (or whatever size the pull bolts are) on the plywood and drill the holes, making sure the holes are perpendicular to the face of the plywood. Attach stops at the top and outer edge of the plywood.

To use the jig on the door of a lower cabinet, push stops against the edge and top end of the door and drill through the holes in the jig. On an upper-cabinet door, push stops against the edge and bottom end.

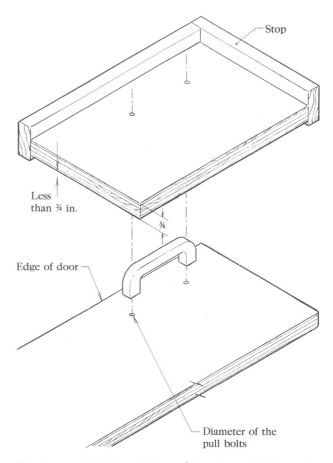

The door-pull jig is made from ¾-in. plywood. To use it, push the stops against the end and the edge of the door, opposite the hinge, then drill the bolt holes as shown.

The drawer-pull jig—Draw a horizontal and a vertical centerline on the top-drawer face. Place the pull so that it straddles the vertical centerline and sits on or slightly above the horizontal centerline, then mark the position of the pull's bolt holes. To make the jig, cut an 8-in. to 10-in.-long piece of ¾-in. plywood nearly as wide as the top-drawer face is long. Transfer the position of the vertical centerline and the bolt holes from the top-drawer face to the plywood, indexing the measurements from one edge. Drill the holes. Extend the centerline onto the edge. Nail a stop to that edge, notched so you'll be able to see the centerline on the jig and on the top edges of the drawer faces, as shown in the drawing below.

To use the jig, mark the center of the top ends of the top-drawer and bottom-drawer faces in a stack. With all the drawers in the cabinet, connect these two marks with a straightedge and make light lines on the top end of each face in between. (If these marks aren't close to the book-match line, you will need to decide whether to center the pulls on the centerline or on the book-match line. Whichever center you choose to use, it is important that the pulls are aligned.)

Place the stop against the top end of the drawer face and then align the two marks in the notch. Drill through the template to make bolt holes for the pull.

(If you use these jigs for a second set of cabinets with different pull locations, be sure to tape over the holes you won't be using—a hole in a jig soon gets a drill through it, and misplaced holes are not easy to fill or patch.)

Magnetic Catches

Some hinges are spring-loaded and self-closing, but many are not, so some cabinet doors may need catches to keep them closed. There is a wide variety of catches to choose from—some mechanical, others magnetic. I prefer the magnetic type because they work nicely and have no moving parts that can wear out or break.

Whatever catch you decide to use should be mounted as close to the pull as possible. It can be fastened to the underside of a fixed shelf, to the side of a partition, or to a wooden block that is glued to a partition, a stile or the back of the top rail or apron rail. I make these blocks about 8 in. long, square or rabbeted to conform to the door style, as shown in the drawing below.

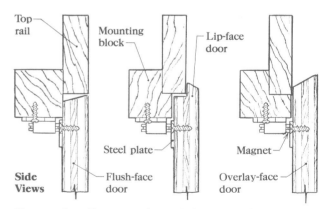

You can install a magnetic catch for doors of any style by gluing a wooden mounting block to the top rail.

Installation of a magnetic catch

1. When mounting the magnet on the cabinet, make sure that you center the screws in the slots to allow for adjustment.

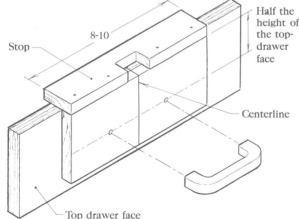

To use the drawer-pull jig, place the jig on the face of the drawer, aligning its centerline with the centerline on the top end of the face.

2. Attach the steel plate to the door by putting a small screw in the plate and positioning both on the magnet, with the screw facing out. Let the door bump lightly into the screw to mark its location, then screw the plate to the door. Use a small drill, nail set, or awl to make a pilot hole for the screw.

3. Adjust the magnet to hold flush-face doors flush with the face frame, and overlay-face and lip-face doors ¹⁄₃₂ in. shy of the face frame.

Installing sink-apron faces— Though the sink-apron face doesn't require special hardware to hold it in place, it's usually mounted at the same time that the doors are hung, so it can be aligned with them.

1. Lip and overlay sink-apron faces are held on the face frame by wooden clips and filler blocks, as shown in the drawing below. An overlay face requires filler blocks of a different thickness than those

for a lip face. The filler should be thin enough so that the clip is sprung slightly into the opening. Rip the clips and fillers about 2½ in. wide. Cut the fillers approximately ¼ in. shorter than the height of the opening, and the clips approximately 1 in. longer.

2. Attach fillers to the back of the face with glue and screws or nails. Screw through each clip and filler into the face, adjusting it to align with neighboring door and drawer faces. Screw it tightly in place.

3. A flush sink-apron face is installed a bit differently. Cut a piece of thin plywood about 1½ in. wider and longer than the face-frame opening. Center the face and glue, screw or nail it on the plywood. Position the sink-apron face in the face-frame opening so the clearance between it and the surrounding rails and stiles matches the clearance around cabinet doors and drawers. Nail or screw through the plywood into the back of the face frame.

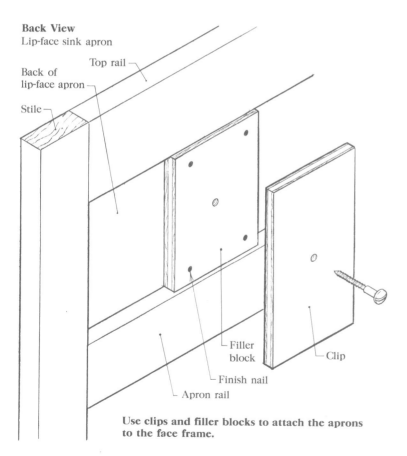

Back View
Lip-face sink apron

Top rail

Back of lip-face apron

Stile

Filler block

Finish nail

Apron rail

Clip

Use clips and filler blocks to attach the aprons to the face frame.

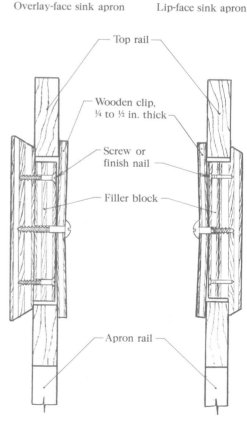

Side Views
Overlay-face sink apron   Lip-face sink apron

Top rail

Wooden clip, ¼ to ½ in. thick

Screw or finish nail

Filler block

Apron rail

Toeboards

Chapter 12

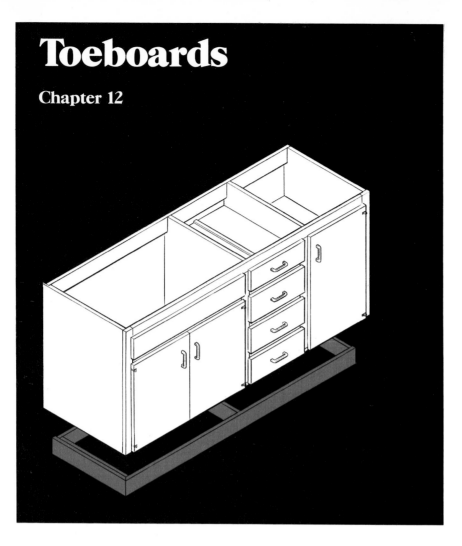

The toeboard (sometimes called the kick plate) creates a toe space that is 3 in. deep and 4 in. high. It allows the user to stand close to the work surface without kicking the drawer or door faces.

Toeboards can be built into the cabinet ends or made as separate frames. I prefer making separate frames because they allow toe space at every face. (A built-in toeboard allows toe space only at the front of the cabinet.) Separate frames also make it easier to level the cabinets on an uneven floor, and they allow a more economical use of materials. When the toeboard is a separate frame, the finish and hidden ends need to be only 31¼ in. long, which means you can cut three ends from the length of a standard-size plywood panel. Building the toeboard into the cabinet

would require cabinet ends that are 35¼ in. long—only two of these can be cut from the length of a plywood panel. Remember, too, if you decided on a face-frame bottom rail wider than ¾ in., the toeboard will have to be wider to compensate (p. 17).

There are four basic toeboard placements, shown on the opposite page. They can meet the wall (or an appliance) on one, two or three sides, or be free-standing. If the toeboard front meets a wall (A), allow extra length for scribing it to the wall. If the toeboard fits between two walls (C), make its front ⅛ in. longer than the opening, and rabbet ⅛ in. into each end for scribing, as shown in the drawing on p. 92. The ends of the toeboard should clear the wall by at least 1½ in. to make it easier to get in place.

End is cut out for toeboard.

A toeboard can be built into the ends of a cabinet, as shown at left, or as a separate frame, as shown below. A separate toeboard acts as a base for the cabinet, making it easier to level the cabinet on an uneven floor.

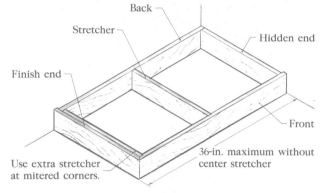

Back

Stretcher

Hidden end

Finish end

Front

Use extra stretcher at mitered corners.

36-in. maximum without center stretcher

This drawing shows top views of four toeboards and how they may be positioned in relation to walls or appliances.

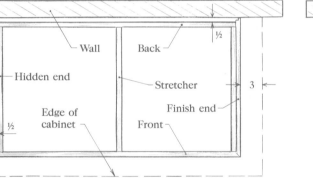

Wall

Back

½

Hidden end

Stretcher

3

Edge of cabinet

Finish end

½

Front

A. Corner Unit

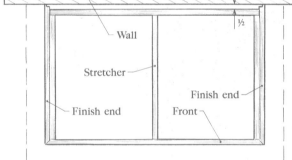

Wall

½

Stretcher

Finish end

Finish end

Front

B. Unit with Both Ends Exposed

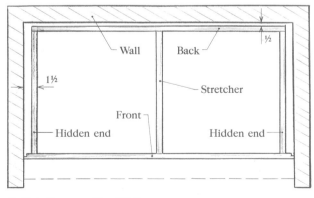

Wall

Back

½

1½

Stretcher

Front

Hidden end

Hidden end

C. Unit Between Two Walls

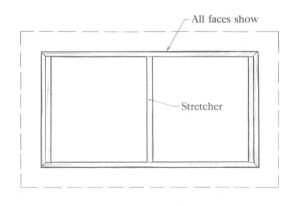

All faces show

Stretcher

D. Island Unit

The hidden end and back of a corner unit, and the back of a unit with both ends exposed should be held away from the walls that run parallel to them by ½ in., as shown in the drawing on p. 91. Where a visible front and end meet, reinforce the miter joint with a stretcher; toeboard frames longer than 36 in. should always be stiffened with a stretcher near the center. If two cabinets meet in a corner, butt the fronts of the toeboards, and leave a ¹⁄₁₆-in. clearance, as shown in the drawing below, so that you'll be able to get a tight joint where the faces meet.

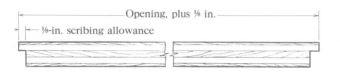

Allow for scribing on toeboards that fit between two walls.

Building a Toeboard

I'll describe how to make a toeboard that meets two walls or appliances (example A on p. 91).

1. First sketch a top view with dimensions to determine the amount of material needed. Then rip enough ¾-in. plywood for all the parts (and an extra long and extra short piece, in case of a mistake.)

2. Butt and rabbet joints leave the plywood edge exposed. Though the edge can be covered with banding, I prefer to use miters where the joints will be visible. (Butt joints are fine where the joints won't show.) Cut the miters on the tablesaw, with its blade tilted to 45°. To check the angle, make a test cut across a piece of scrap, put the two halves together and check the miter with a square. If the halves don't form a right angle, adjust the blade. Also check to see that the mitered ends are square to the edges; adjust the saw's miter gauge if necessary.

Top View

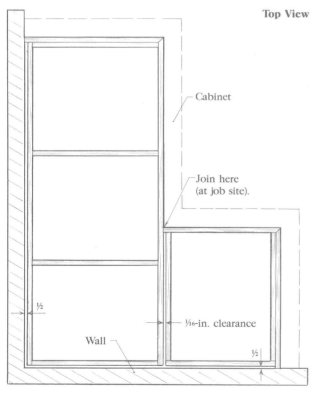

Position toeboards meeting in a corner as shown.

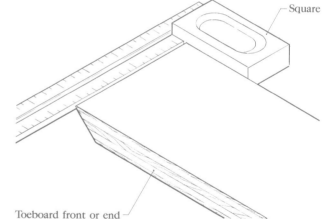

Check to be sure the mitered end is square to the edge.

3. Miter the ends of the mating pieces and the extra pieces. Then, set the saw back to 90° and cut these pieces to length. Usually, there is so little scribing to be done that no extra length is necessary.

4. Lay out the back, hidden end and stretchers on the mitered pieces, and cut the back to length. Then, set up a stop block on the cutoff box and cut the hidden end and stretchers to length.

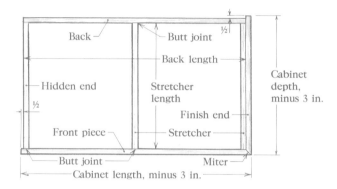

After mitering, lay out the back, hidden end and stretchers, and then cut them to length.

5. Assemble the toeboard into subassemblies. Attach a stretcher to the finish end with glue and 3d nails. (Align the stretcher end with the heel of the miter, or the miter won't close.) Place the front and back together to mark the position of the hidden end and stretcher on each, then glue and nail them to the back. Clamp the finish end (with stretcher attached) to the bench, then glue and nail on the front.

6. Apply glue and nail the two subassemblies together, then check the completed toeboard for square. Nail a piece of scrap diagonally across the toeboard to hold it square while the glue dries. Sand the miters immediately, so that the sawdust will mix with the wet glue to help fill small gaps in the miter.

Countertop Underlayment

Chapter 13

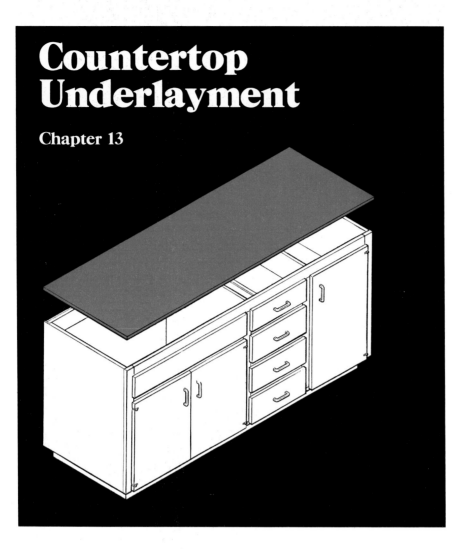

Kitchen counters consist of ¾-in.-thick plywood or particleboard underlayment, to which is attached the countertop surface. The underlayment is usually edge-banded with ¾-in.-thick solid wood along all visible edges. The underlayment and banding allow the countertop to overhang the cabinet by 1 in., as shown in the drawing on the opposite page. The underlayment must be cut longer and wider than the cabinet, to allow for the overhang and for scribing to the walls. (If the finish end of a cabinet fits against an appliance, the overhang is usually eliminated.) The underlayment and countertop are attached to the cabinets after installation, but the underlayment edges are banded before. You can leave off the banding, but you'll lose the illusion of a thick countertop.

Making the Underlayment

1. Begin by ripping the plywood to width, then cut it to length. Don't forget that the underlayment must be longer and wider than the case to allow for scribing and for the countertop overhang. To make scribing easier, I cut a ¼-in. by ½-in. rabbet on the underside of the underlayment edges that meet the walls. When cutting the underlayment for cabinets that meet in a corner, tie the units together by overlapping the joint where the cabinets meet, as shown on the opposite page. (If you were to put the underlayment joint directly over the joint where the units meet, it would probably open as the house settled.) To support the joint, glue and nail a ¾-in. piece of

plywood, about 4 in. wide, to the cabinet through the face frame and back; then glue and nail the underlayment to the plywood. If you're using a plastic-laminate or tile countertop surface, this support piece will keep the counter from cracking at the joint.

2. Make the bandings. I prefer bandings 1¼ in. wide, but they can range from 1 in. to 1½ in.—any wider and the top rail of the face frame will look too narrow. Joint and rip the bandings from straight-grained wood, as discussed on p. 30. Knots make it hard to plane the banding flush with the underlayment. If the banding will be covered with plastic laminate on its top edge and face, you can use a softwood such as pine, but if the face of the banding will show, the wood should match the cabinet face.

3. Cut the bandings to length, and then glue and nail them to the underlayment. If the banding faces will not be covered with plastic laminate, miter the bandings on outside corners so end grain won't show; use butt joints everywhere else. Put the jointed edge of each band down and hold the sawn edge flush, or about ¼₄ in. above the underlayment top. Use glue and a 6d nail positioned about every 12 in. to fasten the bandings to the underlayment. (When attaching hardwood bands, use clamps to avoid nail holes.)

4. Finally, plane the bandings flush with the underlayment. Don't bevel them, or the countertop won't be evenly supported.

Now you're ready to transport the cabinets to the kitchen and install them.

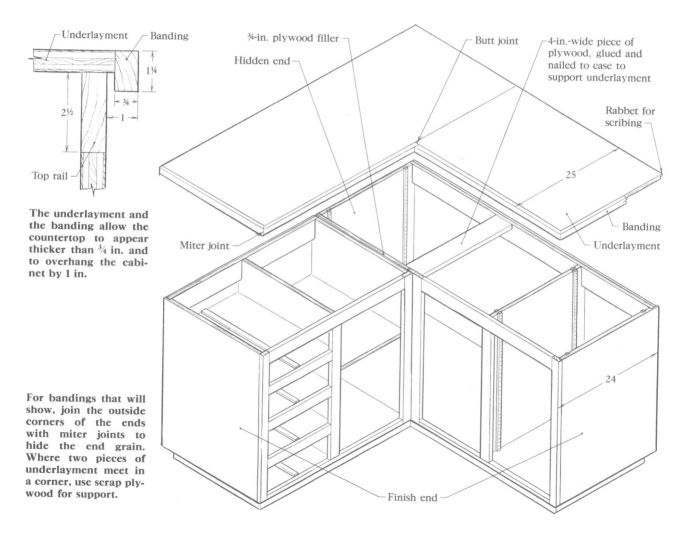

The underlayment and the banding allow the countertop to appear thicker than ¾ in. and to overhang the cabinet by 1 in.

For bandings that will show, join the outside corners of the ends with miter joints to hide the end grain. Where two pieces of underlayment meet in a corner, use scrap plywood for support.

Cabinet Installation

Chapter 14

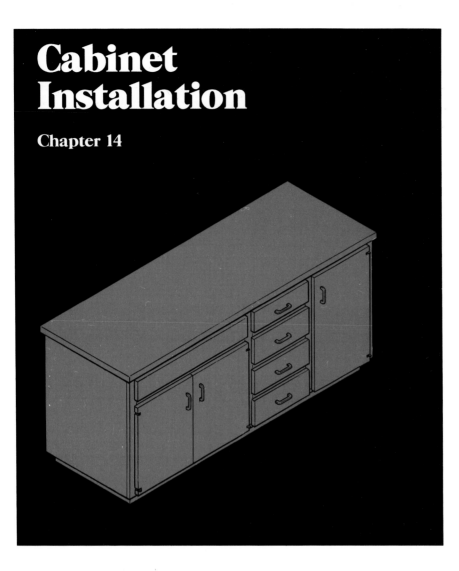

The first step in installation is setting up the toe-boards. Lower cabinets are added to the toeboards next, and upper cabinets attached to the wall last. Installation is the moment of truth. At times you may doubt that everything is going to fit, but don't worry—if the story-stick layout was done accurately and the cabinets built according to the sticks, the cabinets will fit just the way they're supposed to.

Installing the Toeboards

In most cases, all there is to setting up a toeboard is leveling it, scribing it to the walls and nailing it to the floor. If you have a toeboard that has to fit be-tween two walls, however, you can't level the toe-board until you've scribed it to fit the space. The special techniques for this are discussed in steps 1 through 3; if you don't have to fit the toeboard be-tween walls, go directly to step 4 to level the toe-board, and then scribe it to the walls as explained in step 1. If cabinets are covered with the same counter-top, or if they butt up to one another (such as in L-shaped or U-shaped kitchens), the toeboards should be fastened together and then leveled as a single unit (p. 92). This will ensure that adjoining countertops are the same height.

1. Twist the toeboard to get one end in place be-tween the walls. On the face of the toeboard at that end, draw a line that is parallel to the wall with a

scriber. (A compass will work fine, too.) Set the scriber so that its gap is the same as the greatest gap between the toeboard and the wall; run the tool's pointer down the wall and its pencil point down the toeboard face. Plane or saw to this line, and the toeboard will fit tightly to any irregularities in the wall.

2. Measure the distance between the walls (4 in. above the floor) and transfer that measurement to the top edge of the unscribed end of the toeboard. Twist the toeboard between the walls so that the marked end is in place.

3. Set the scriber to the distance between the wall and the mark, and then scribe the toeboard face. Plane or saw to within $\frac{1}{16}$ in. and test the fit. Remove a little wood at a time and keep checking until the toeboard fits perfectly.

4. Level the toeboard using slim wedges. (Wooden shingles work well for this.) Fasten the wedges to wooden floors with small nails; for concrete floors, use construction adhesive—a heavy, gap-filling adhesive. (Imagine how difficult leveling would be if the toeboard were fastened to the cabinet.)

5. If the toeboard doesn't have to be fitted between two walls, scribe it to the walls after leveling.

6. Toenail the toeboard to the floor with a few 6d or 8d nails or use construction adhesive. If any wedges were used at the front or finish end, be sure to cut them off flush with the toeboard face using a knife, chisel or handsaw. Hide the wedges with molding after the floor covering is installed.

Installing the Lower Cabinets

1. Begin by placing the lower unit on the toeboard. Move it against the wall—without a doubt, there will be gaps where the finish end and the face frame meet the walls. Set the scriber so that its gap is equal to the greatest gap between the cabinet and wall, and run it down the back edge of the finish end. Do the same to the face frame at the hidden end.

2. Now slide the cabinet away from the wall and plane to the scribed line with a block plane. Hold the plane at an angle to bevel the joint back from the face, so that it will fit tightly to the wall.

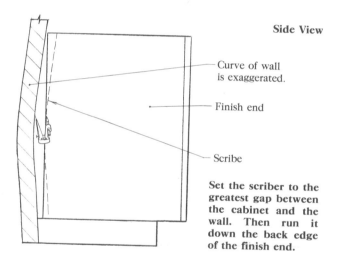

Side View

Curve of wall is exaggerated.

Finish end

Scribe

Set the scriber to the greatest gap between the cabinet and the wall. Then run it down the back edge of the finish end.

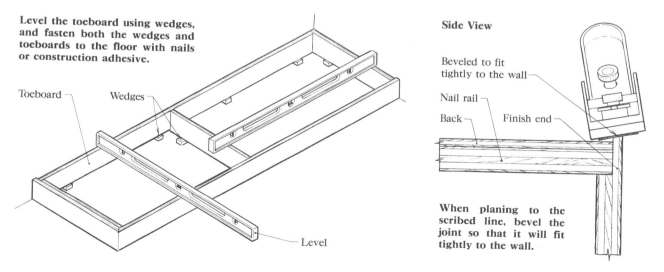

Level the toeboard using wedges, and fasten both the wedges and toeboards to the floor with nails or construction adhesive.

Toeboard

Wedges

Level

Side View

Beveled to fit tightly to the wall

Nail rail

Back

Finish end

When planing to the scribed line, bevel the joint so that it will fit tightly to the wall.

3. After planing, try the cabinet in place. Each scribed part should fit tightly against the wall without much pressure. If it takes a lot of pressure, you're probably twisting the cabinet, which may eventually cause it to sag away from the wall. Plane a bit more off until the cabinet fits, and you are ready to fasten it to the wall.

4. Locate the studs in the wall, drop wedges between the cabinet and wall, and start nails through the nail rail and the back edge of the hidden end. The wedges fill the gap (created by the scribing allowance) between the nail rail or hidden end and wall. You can use 8d box nails or screws, but screws should be long enough to anchor about 1 in. into the stud. Open the doors and start more nails near the bottom. If you can find a stud, try to get a pair of nails (top and bottom) near the front edge of the hidden end. Before driving the nails home, check the fit. If it's still okay, finish driving the nails. The last nails started—the ones without the wedges behind them—

should be driven flush with the wood using good, solid blows. Driving with light blows, or driving after the head is set flush, will only break the joint between the back and the finish end, or between the hidden end and the face frame or bottom. Several 6d finish nails through the bottom and into the front of the toeboard should complete the fastening. Trim off the top ends of the wedges with a handsaw. Cabinets that fit together end to end, or that form an *L*, should be attached to each other with several screws or bolts.

5. A cabinet that fits between two walls requires special scribing techniques. Remember that one stile of its face frame should have been left unglued. Scribe the attached stile to the wall as described in steps 1 and 2, set the cabinet back in place and attach it to the wall. Now clamp the loose stile over the top of the rails so that it is parallel to the attached stile. Set the scriber for the amount that the stile overlaps the rails and scribe the stile to the wall.

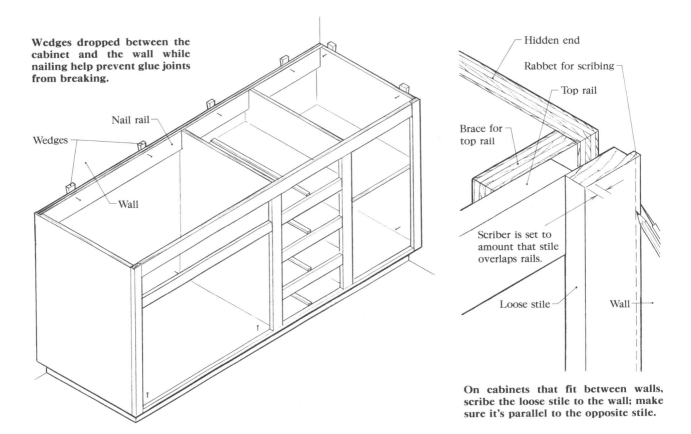

Wedges dropped between the cabinet and the wall while nailing help prevent glue joints from breaking.

Nail rail

Wedges

Wall

Hidden end

Rabbet for scribing

Top rail

Brace for top rail

Scriber is set to amount that stile overlaps rails.

Loose stile

Wall

On cabinets that fit between walls, scribe the loose stile to the wall; make sure it's parallel to the opposite stile.

Plane or saw close to the line, testing for fit as you go. When you're sure the fit is right, glue and nail the loose stile in place.

6. When all the lower cabinets are attached to the wall, put the underlayment in place and scribe it to the wall. It's not necessary that the underlayment be scribed absolutely tight to the wall—most counter materials will bridge a gap of $\frac{1}{16}$ in. or less. (The underlayment should fit tightly, however, where its bandings meet the wall.)

7. Use white or yellow glue and 6d finish nails to fasten the underlayment in place. Be sure to set the nails. (However, if you're planning a full plastic-laminate backsplash, as discussed on p. 101, don't attach the underlayment now.) Nail the underlayment to the nail rail, ends, partitions and the top rail of the face frame. Place a heavy object (a maul or axhead) under the top rail to support it while nailing. If the cabinet has a breadboard, be careful not to nail into it.

Installing the Upper Cabinets

1. Once the lower units are in place, install the uppers. (If you're going to use the full plastic-laminate backsplash, you can avoid difficulty scribing by installing it before hanging the upper cabinet, as discussed on p. 101.) A couple of simple support boxes placed on the underlayment will help position the upper cabinets at the correct height, as shown in the drawing below. Make the boxes at least $\frac{3}{4}$ in. shorter

than the distance between the underlayment and the bottom of the upper unit. (Taller supports will get trapped in place after the cabinet is installed.) Raise the boxes to the right height with shims.

2. If the upper cabinets are to be scribed to the ceiling, level them and mark them with a scriber. When the fit is right, scribe the finish end and face frame to the walls.

3. Fasten the upper cabinets to the wall the same way you did the lowers. Try to get a nail or long screw through the nail rail into at least every other stud. Drive a few more nails or screws through the back and hidden end, about two-thirds of the way down the cabinet, to hold the bottom to the wall. If the shelves are fixed, hide these fasteners by putting them just above the shelves that are above eye level, or below shelves that are below eye level.

4. If the upper cabinets don't need to be scribed to the ceiling, toenail nails down through the top into the studs for extra strength. These nails must bite into the top enough to keep them from tearing out, so use 8d or 10d nails.

Another way to hang uppers that won't be scribed to the ceiling is shown in the drawing below. The wall must be relatively straight to use this method. Rip one piece of $\frac{1}{4}$-in. plywood into two at approximately a 45° angle. Anchor one piece of plywood to the cabinet with glue and nails; anchor the second piece to the wall. Hang the cabinet on this second piece; put in a few nails to keep it from swinging away from the wall.

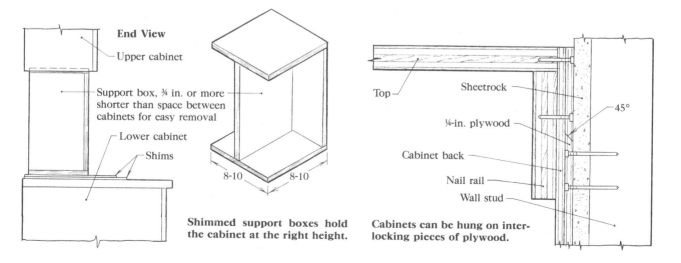

End View

Upper cabinet

Support box, ¾ in. or more shorter than space between cabinets for easy removal

Lower cabinet

Shims

8-10   8-10

Shimmed support boxes hold the cabinet at the right height.

Top

Sheetrock

45°

¼-in. plywood

Cabinet back

Nail rail

Wall stud

Cabinets can be hung on interlocking pieces of plywood.

Countertop Surfaces

Chapter 15

The countertop is one of the most important parts of a kitchen cabinet. You can choose from a variety of materials—wood, tile, natural or synthetic marble and plastic laminate. I'll discuss each of these, but in general, when choosing countertop material, pay attention to appearance, the initial cost of the material compared to its life expectancy, and the special skills and tools necessary to install it. Maintenance is another concern: work surfaces should be either resistant to damage, or easy to refurbish.

Wood countertops add richness to a kitchen, and many cooks prefer to work on wood. Though these countertops can be easily scratched, they can be maintained by periodic sanding followed by a good rubbing with mineral oil. When wood is used as a countertop surface, it is most often in the form of laminated pieces of maple. These laminated tops are available at many lumber supply houses, but some craftsmen prefer to glue up their own.

Laminated wood tops are usually thicker than ¾ in., and the extra thickness should be calculated into the layout of the vertical story stick. The underside of the top must be at least 34½ in. above the floor to clear a dishwasher, and the countertop surface should be about 36 in. from the floor. Screw laminated wood tops to the cabinet through nail rails attached face up at the front and back of the case (p. 10).

Ceramic tile over exterior plywood underlayment has long been a popular countertop surface. Tile is heat-resistant, and can be used in the cooking area without fear of its being damaged by hot pans. You'll notice some wear on the glaze eventually, but damaged tiles can be replaced, as can the grout between them. A few specialized tools are needed for scribing and cutting the tile, but these can be rented from a supply house or a tool-rental agency. Just about anyone with the interest, moderate skill and a good how-to book (such as the one listed in the bibliography) can do a good job installing tile.

Marble secured to the underlayment with mastic makes a durable, beautiful countertop. However, marble is expensive, and cutting and finishing it requires special skills and equipment. (Some people install marble on just a small portion of the countertop, as a special surface for cooling candy or kneading bread.) When using marble, calculate its thickness into the cabinet height to ensure room for a dishwasher. (Marble countertops are usually ¾ in. to 1¼ in. thick.)

Synthetic marble is a type of plastic that is close to natural marble in looks and durability. Most synthetic marbles can be cut and worked with common woodworking tools. They come in sheets that are 30 in. wide and 6 ft., 8 ft. or 10 ft. long. Available thicknesses are ¼ in., ½ in. and ¾ in. When glued over an underlayment, a thickness of ½ in. is adequate.

Plastic laminate, which is the countertop surface I will discuss here, is one of the most popular materials. It is relatively inexpensive, and because it comes in sheets up to 60 in. by 144 in., large areas can be covered without seams. The choice of colors and textures is vast—there's a laminate to complement just about any decor. The material is durable and resists heat to nearly 300°F, but because the color layer is thin, scratches are nearly impossible to repair. Though installing plastic laminate requires several special skills, these are within the range of anyone with interest and patience. No special tools are required, as the laminate can be cut with common woodworking tools.

Before working with plastic laminate, you must consider the following questions:

How much backsplash should there be, and when should it be applied?
A backsplash puts a durable, easily cleaned surface on the wall behind the counter to catch spills and splashes. There are two approaches to backsplash in-stallation, depending on whether you use a full backsplash or partial backsplash.

A full backsplash covers the entire wall between the upper and lower cabinets. It is usually installed before the underlayment is nailed to the lower cabinet and before the upper cabinet is in place. After the upper cabinet is installed, the underlayment is nailed down, the banding on its edge covered with laminate (if desired), and the countertop installed.

Partial backsplashes usually run 4 in. to 12 in. up the wall. I usually use them instead of full backsplashes because they're easier to install. If you're using a partial backsplash, install the cabinets first, nail down the underlayment, cover its banding with laminate if you wish, then put on the countertop. Finish with the backsplash.

If the cabinets have been installed and you want a full backsplash, you must scribe it to fit between the upper and lower cabinets. This is hard to do, but fitting can be made easier by using metal moldings. But cutting and fitting the moldings requires careful work, too. Cove molding is used where the backsplash joins the countertop, and cap molding adds a decorative detail to the top edge and exposed end.

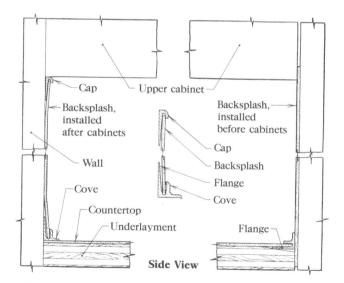

Aluminum cap moldings can be positioned on the top edge of full or partial backsplashes; cove moldings can be positioned where the backsplash meets the countertop. File away some of the flange before installing, to keep it from forcing the laminate away from the underlayment or wall.

How should the countertop edge be treated?

The banding on the underlayment may either be left exposed or covered with laminate (which is called a self edge). If you leave the band exposed, you might rout a detail on the top front corner with a beveled laminate-trimmer bit or a cove bit. This detail is not only decorative, but puts the tender edge of the laminate out of the way of most damaging blows. The router base will prevent the detail from running all the way to a wall, so file the last 3 in. or so of laminate flush with the face of the band.

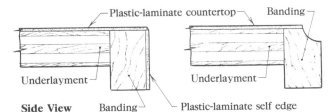

Side View

The underlayment edge band can either be left exposed or covered with plastic laminate. If left exposed, a routed detail adds a decorative touch.

Where should you place the laminate seams?

The obvious answer is: wherever they will be least noticeable—for example, centered on either or both sides of a sink or countertop-range opening. A seam is also acceptable in the corner of an *L*-shaped counter. If the laminate has a random pattern, run the seam parallel to either edge of the counter; if the pattern is symmetrical, the seam should be mitered at the corner so that the pattern runs parallel to the front and back edges of the counter. Prevent seams from opening by placing them at least 4 in. away from joints in the underlayment.

How should the laminate be cut?

Laminate can usually be ordered in pieces as small as 24 in. by 24 in. Sizes increase in increments of 12 in. to a maximum sheet size of 60 in. by 144 in. When ordering, try to buy one or two large sheets to minimize waste. Plan to rough-cut the pieces ⅜ in. to ¾ in. oversized—they will be trimmed to exact size after they're attached to the underlayment.

Plastic laminate can be rough-cut with a handsaw or tablesaw, or by scoring the face with a carbide-tipped scoring tool made for plastic laminate. Then the score is snapped, the same way you'd break a piece of glass. Scoring is difficult to do, so I recommend sawing. All saws will chip the laminate somewhat, but by trimming the pieces to exact size with a router after installation, you can eliminate the chipped edge. If you are using a tablesaw, keep the laminate from slipping under the rip fence by placing a strip of ¼-in. plywood next to the fence and under the laminate. Keep the plywood from sliding forward by driving a long nail in one end to act as a stop against the saw table.

A small amount (¼ in. or less) can be trimmed from the edge of a piece of laminate with a pair of tin snips, without chipping or fracturing the face of the wide piece. But the narrow piece will always be badly fractured.

What kind of adhesives should be used?

While most adhesives will adhere to the back side of laminate, they require extremely high pressure for extended periods of time. Contact cement also requires high pressure, but only for a fraction of a second, and adequate pressure can be exerted with a hard rubber roller or a hammer and block of wood. Every brand of contact cement is made a little differently, so be sure to read and follow the instructions on the label.

Contact cement must be applied to each mating surface and allowed to dry for approximately 10 to 30 minutes before the surfaces are put together. Once the pieces touch, they lock, which means that it's important to get the plastic laminate in place correctly on the first try. This is one reason plastic laminate is applied oversized: slight errors in placement can be corrected in the trimming process. When metal cap and cove moldings are to be used on a backsplash, the backsplash must be the last piece applied, so it is usually held in place with cohesive mastic to allow it to be positioned correctly.

How should you trim the plastic laminate?

A router with a straight laminate-trimmer bit will cut plastic laminate with practically no chipping. A sharp mill bastard file will remove any marks left by the router. The file is also used in corners where the router won't reach. Where two pieces of laminate meet at 90°, you'll also need a beveled laminate-trimmer bit to bevel the edges.

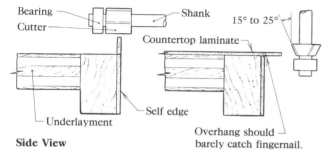

Side View

Use the straight trimmer on the self edge, then the beveled trimmer on the countertop. File off the small overhang.

Installing the Countertop

Applying plastic laminate requires a number of specialized methods. I'll explain how to install a plastic-laminate countertop with a partial backsplash.

1. Rough-cut the laminate for the countertop, self edge and backsplash, adding ⅜ in. to each edge that will be trimmed after the laminate is installed.

2. Fasten the self edge to the banding on the underlayment, if desired. Doing this before applying the countertop puts the joint on the vertical surface, which looks good and keeps spills out, as shown in the drawing below. Scribe the end of the self edge to the wall and trim it with a file. The top and bottom edges are trimmed with a router after installation. However, because the router base makes it impossi-

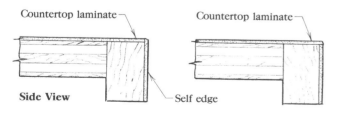

Side View

Attach the self edge before the countertop laminate to keep spills out of the joint.

ble to trim all the way to the wall, cut away about 3 in. of the self edge closest to the wall before applying it. Make it about ⅟₁₆ in. over the band width, and file off the extra after installation.

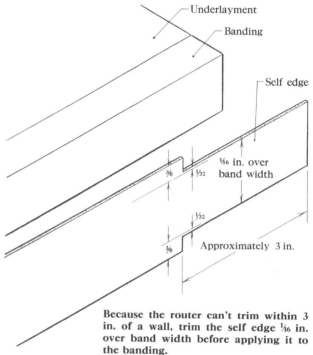

Because the router can't trim within 3 in. of a wall, trim the self edge ⅟₁₆ in. over band width before applying it to the banding.

3. Apply contact cement to the self edge and the band, let the cement dry, then put the self edge in place. Take care to apply the laminate so it overhangs the band at the top and bottom. Roll or tap it with a hammer and block of wood to seat it well.

4. Trim the self edge with the router and a straight bit. The bearing will ride on the top and bottom edges of the band as the cutter trims the plastic laminate flush with them.

5. The router will leave mill marks and a hump wherever the bearing on the bit rolls over a chip. Remove these with a few strokes of a sharp file. Hold the toe of the file on the underlayment to prevent beveling the top edge of the laminate.

6. Repeat the procedure described in steps 2 through 5 for each piece of self edge.

7. Install the countertop. If two pieces of laminate are needed to cover the entire counter, you'll need to prepare the seam. Good-looking, tight seams can be made using the router and the following method.

Clamp one piece of the laminate to be seamed to a piece of plywood, one edge flush with the plywood edge. Locate the second piece flush with the same plywood edge and a little less than ¾ in. (or the width of whatever straight router bit you use) from the first piece. Use the bit gauge (p. 121) to position a straightedge so that the router will trim a little off both pieces of laminate. Set the router bit just deep enough to cut through the laminate, and trim both pieces with one cut, as shown in the top drawing at right. (If you slip a scrap of laminate in between the plywood and the laminate when you're setting up, you can avoid grooving the plywood.) Then dull the sharp edges of both pieces with a very fine file to prevent the edges from chipping when forced together. Use one light stroke, holding the file at about 45° to the face of the laminate. Using the same technique, you can trim the mitered seam for two pieces that meet in a corner of an *L*-shaped counter.

If you find that one piece of laminate is slightly thicker than the other, correct the problem by applying one or two extra coats of contact cement on the thin piece during the cementing process. When making a seam, be careful not to get any cement on the mating edges of the laminate, because the glue will hold the pieces apart slightly and make the seam more noticeable.

8. Now you're ready to scribe the countertop to the back wall. Tin snips and a file will do the job if there isn't much material to remove; use a router, bit gauges and clamps if there's a lot. The gauges position the laminate so the router can use the wall as a guide to trim it to fit exactly. Put the gauges against the wall and place the laminate so the router will trim about ⅛ in., as shown in the bottom drawing at right. To avoid cutting into the underlayment and self edge at the finish end, slip a piece of scrap laminate under the piece to be trimmed. Set the bit to just cut through the thickness of the countertop laminate. Hold the router tightly against the wall and move from right to left—the cut will match every irregularity in the wall. (If the countertop butts into a wall, trim the last few inches with tin snips and a file.)

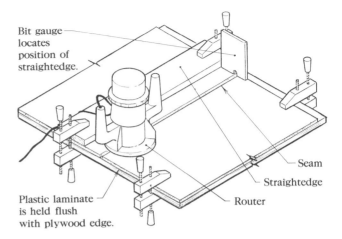

Bit gauge locates position of straightedge.

Plastic laminate is held flush with plywood edge.

Seam

Straightedge

Router

Use this setup for seaming two pieces of plastic laminate.

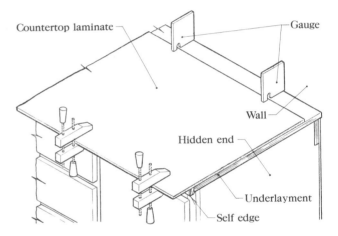

Countertop laminate

Gauge

Wall

Hidden end

Underlayment

Self edge

Use this setup for scribing the countertop to the back wall.

9. If the cabinet is between two walls, both ends and the back edge will need to be scribed. To do this, place a piece of building paper (tar paper) that is slightly smaller than the top on the underlayment. With the pencil leg of the scriber against each wall and the point on the paper, scribe the paper. Now place the paper on the laminate. Using the same setting on the scriber, put the pencil point on the laminate and the other point on the scribe line on the paper, and mark the laminate. Trim to the scribe line, and the laminate should fit perfectly.

10. Apply the cement to laminate and underlayment, as directed on the container, and let it dry.

11. Prepare to position the laminate on the underlayment. The cemented surfaces will grab, so place strips of scrap laminate or metal on the underlayment to allow you to adjust the laminate correctly. These strips must be absolutely clean, so that they won't leave particles in the cement.

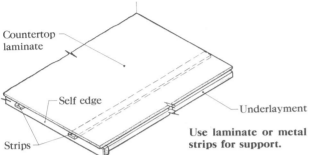

Use laminate or metal strips for support.

to length. File off sharp edges if no cap molding will be used; if you're using a cap molding, fit it to the exposed edges of the laminate now. Cap molding can be cut and mitered with a hacksaw on an outside corner, or a 90° notch can be removed from the flange and the molding bent to form the corner.

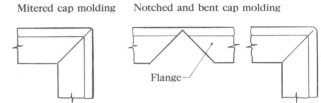

Fit the cap molding on corners by mitering or bending it.

When you're sure the laminate is in the proper place, gently pull the center strip out and press the laminate down so the two surfaces lock. Pull the strips out one at a time, working from the center to the ends. At the same time, roll the laminate toward the ends so no air gets trapped underneath.

12. To trim the laminate on the finish end and front, set up the router with a beveled laminate-trimmer bit. Bit depth is important here—the correct depth will leave just enough of the top overhanging the self edge to catch a fingernail on, as shown in the drawing on p. 103. (The ball bearing runs against the self edge, and if you set the bit too deep, it will cut part of the self edge away.) Try the cut on scrap first.

13. Trim all the edges, filing away the extra near the walls. Remove the overhang left by the bit with a fine file or chisel. (Drag the flat side of a sharp chisel across a piece of 400-grit, wet/dry sandpaper at about a 15° angle, to remove any burrs and keep the chisel from digging in.)

14. Use a fine file to remove the router marks. Hold it at the same angle as the bevel (15° to 25°). To remove any sharp edges, hold the file at about 45° to the face and use one or two long strokes. Use a very light stroke to ease any outside corners on the countertop. Don't file too much—a stroke or two will do.

15. Now prepare the backsplash. Scribe the end that fits against the wall, then finish-cut the laminate

16. If you're using a cove molding, cut and fit it before cementing on the backsplash—the molding has to fit behind the last piece of laminate put down. Removing some of the molding's flange will help prevent it from forcing the laminate away from the underlayment or the wall, as shown in the drawing on p. 101. If you're not using a cove molding, scribe the splash to the countertop and file the exposed edge to remove sharp corners.

17. Mark the wall about ⅛ in. from the top edge and exposed end of the splash to show where the contact cement (or cohesive mastic) should be applied. Apply the cement to the wall and backsplash, with the molding in place (if you're using molding). When the cement has dried, carefully put the backsplash in place. Roll it or tap it with a hammer and a block of wood to seat the laminate on the wall.

18. The last step is to clean up the countertop with lacquer thinner or the thinner recommended on the label of the contact cement.

With age, the laminate may pull loose from the underlayment. Sometimes the heat from an iron or small propane torch is enough to reactivate the contact cement. But take care not to scorch the laminate—you want just the degree of heat your hand can tolerate, no more. Then roll the laminate or clamp it in place. You can also use this method to remove a piece of laminate from the underlayment.

Finishing Materials

Chapter 16

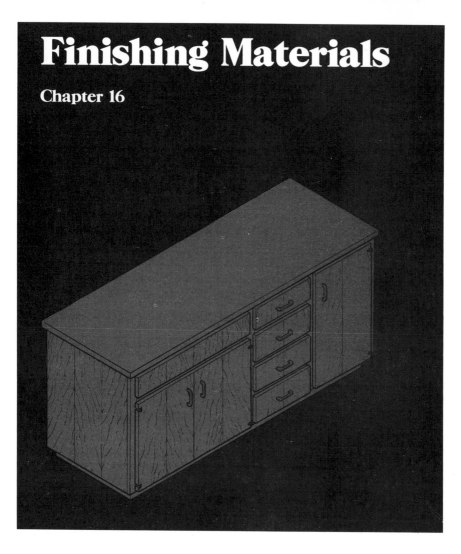

I love woodworking, but not wood finishing. When I have to do it, I prefer to use a penetrating oil; for kitchen cabinets, I choose one made for exterior finishes. Penetrating oil soaks into the wood's pores, leaving only a slight amount on the surface. Though they tend to darken the wood, oils let the wood's natural beauty shine through. (Built-up finishes, such as varnish and lacquer, leave a glassy surface.)

Oil is easy to apply, and each subsequent coat adds to the richness of the finish. After wiping down the freshly sanded surface of the wood with a tack rag, or sweeping it off with a good brush, flood the surface with oil, let it soak in for 10 to 15 minutes, then sand with 400-grit, wet/dry paper. Wipe off the excess, then polish the surface with a dry cloth.

Though most modern penetrating oils are made to harden within the pores (a process called polymerization), they're less water-resistant than built-up finishes. But if you use enough coats, an oil finish is surprisingly resistant to stains and spills. For kitchen cabinets, I recommend at least three coats, with at least 12 hours allowed between applications. If an oil finish is damaged, it's easy to repair: just sand out the damaged area and rub in more finish.

Unlike oils, built-up finishes sit on top of the wood, so they provide good protection. But they're hard to repair, so if they get damaged, you may have to sand and refinish the entire surface. I usually use a built-up finish only when I'm adding cabinets to a kitchen and have to match the existing finish.

Built-up finishes usually consist of an undercoat and a topcoat. The undercoat can be a sealer, stain or filler, or a combination of these. (The order in which the components of the undercoat are applied varies with each situation, so check a good book for guidelines. Two books are listed in the bibliography.) The topcoat is usually varnish or lacquer. Plan out all the steps and products you'll use at the same time, because not all finishing materials are compatible. Check the can for precautions.

If you want a built-up finish, begin by raising the grain. Wipe the wood quickly with a damp cloth to cause the wood fibers to spring up, then sand them off with 400-grit to 600-grit paper. (If you don't sand, the fibers will stick up through the finish.) When the wood has dried, wipe it down with a tack rag, and you're ready to apply the undercoat.

Sealers—Sealers lessen the absorption of the more-expensive topcoat finish, and also help the wood absorb stain uniformly; sealing is especially important if you'll be staining birch or alder, both of which tend to blotch. Some sealers hold the wood fibers down so subsequent coats of finish won't raise the grain, others hold the fibers up so they can be sanded off. Sanding sealers (which have a lacquer base) raise the grain and must be lightly sanded after application; you don't have to sand oil sealers (which have an oil base). In addition, oil sealers make the grain patterns of the wood appear deeper and richer than they do with sanding sealers.

Stains—Stains change the color of the wood, accent its grain patterns and even out uneven coloring. But staining is like stepping off a cliff—once you're over, you can't go back—so test the stain on a piece of scrap first. Apply the stain over the sealer (if you use one), let it dry until the desired color is reached, and then wipe the surface with a rag. Let the stain dry and continue with the finish.

Fillers—Pastewood fillers are used to fill the pores of open-grained woods, such as ash, walnut and oak, before a built-up finish is applied. As with stains, try fillers on scrap first to be sure of the color and effect.

For small checks, gaps at a joint or nail holes, use putty that remains plastic after drying. (It's available in stick form.) Work it in with a small, flat blade just before the last coat of finish. You don't need to sand, but wipe off any excess with a cloth.

Plastic Wood, which dries hard, is good for filling large knotholes or splits in the veneer of interior cabinet parts. Put it on before any finish is applied, and sand it flush with the surrounding wood after it dries. Stain will accent Plastic Wood, so any patches will be slightly noticeable.

Topcoats—Once the undercoat has been applied, you are ready to apply a topcoat of varnish or lacquer (both are available in high, medium or flat gloss). Of the varieties of varnish, polyurethane gives the hardest finish, but it yellows when exposed to sunlight. Of the lacquers, synthetic lacquers (catalyzed or latex) are the most protective, but these require special spraying equipment for their application. I don't recommend regular lacquer (nitrocellulose) for kitchen work—it's not resistant enough to water and grease.

Finishing Tips

Any type of finishing material will highlight glue and scratches, so a good finish begins with sanding. Use paper just coarse enough to remove the worst scratches, and progress to 150 grit or 220 grit. (Sanding with finer paper will only burnish the wood and make it difficult for some finishes to adhere.) This sanding should be done by hand, parallel to the grain. After sanding, vacuum up the dust so that the workshop is clean for finishing.

Be sure to finish both sides of the cabinet doors, otherwise the doors are likely to warp. (You don't have to finish both sides of parts like the cabinet bottom and hidden end, because they're restrained from warping by other parts.) Finish the bottom edges of the doors and finish ends too, or the unfinished surfaces will allow moisture in the air (from a dishwasher, for example) to penetrate, which will cause the face veneer to streak.

I usually finish wooden countertops and breadboards with several coats of mineral oil. Though mineral oil doesn't offer much protection to the wood, it is nontoxic, and suitable for surfaces that come in contact with food.

Jigs and Fixtures

Chapter 17

Table Saw - 36" High

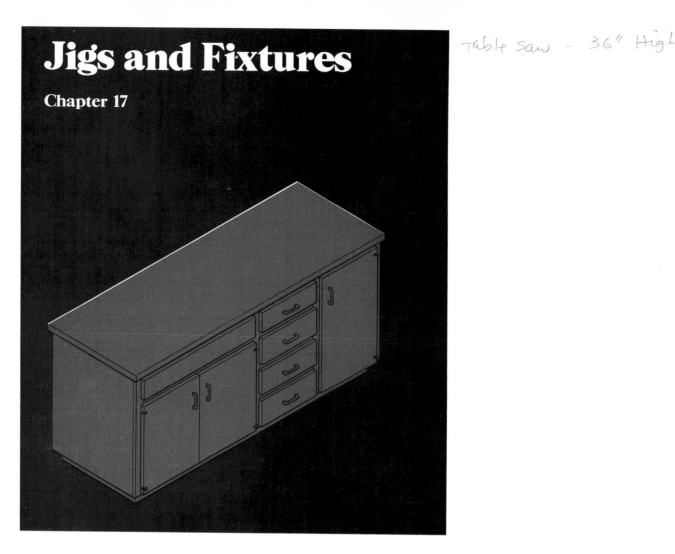

Jigs and fixtures are devices that are used with hand and power tools to improve the accuracy and increase the speed of an operation, to make duplicate parts easily, and to ensure safety—in other words, to help the craftsman make more efficient use of time and equipment. Though some jigs and fixtures are so specialized that they may be of only limited use, the six discussed here have a variety of uses, and should enhance most woodworking shops.

The roller support is used to support long or awkward pieces. Its height is adjustable, so it can be used with a number of machines. The cutoff box, which is used on the tablesaw to crosscut wide pieces accurately, will take the full width of a sheet of plywood. (The miter cutoff box is rather specialized, but it is handy for cutting miters on boards up to 3 in. wide.) The roller support and cutoff box are often used together. The roller takes the weight of the box as it comes off the saw and keeps it from tipping, preventing injury to the operator and damage to the work or cutoff box.

The last three devices extend the versatility of the router. Bit gauges make setting up for a cut easy, quick and accurate. The shaper table allows the work to be moved over the router, and is useful for making moldings and for routing pieces of small dimensions. The edge-band trimmer makes fast work of trimming lots of edge-banded parts and it will also trim cross-grained or curly-grained bandings with a minimum of tear-out.

Roller Support

The roller support is practically indispensable and should be one of the first fixtures that you make. It should be stable so that it won't tip over easily, and the height of the roller should be adjustable so that it can be used with several different machines and accommodate slight irregularities in the shop floor. The roller should turn easily and not be tapered, or it will lead the material sideways as it passes over the roller. (You can buy roller components from caster supply or materials-handling houses, but I'll describe how to make them yourself.)

The roller should be solid wood, but the stand can be made of solid wood or hardwood plywood. If the roller support is to be used in the home shop, primarily behind a tablesaw, ¾-in. material will be adequate for the stand. For a commercial shop or school shop, use thicker material for the feet (up to 1½ in.); the support will be subject to more use and abuse, and the extra weight near the floor will reduce the chance of tipping.

Tailor the height and width of the roller support to your shop. Measure the table height of the various machines with which it may be used (jointer, tablesaw, radial arm saw, bandsaw), and the height of your workbench. The difference between the highest and lowest surfaces determines the range of adjustment that you'll need. If this range is greater than 8 in. or 10 in., the stand may be unstable, and you should consider making two roller stands of different heights. Make the stand for the tablesaw first. The roller for the tablesaw support should be from 30 in. to 36 in. long so that it can easily carry the 48-in.-wide cutoff box.

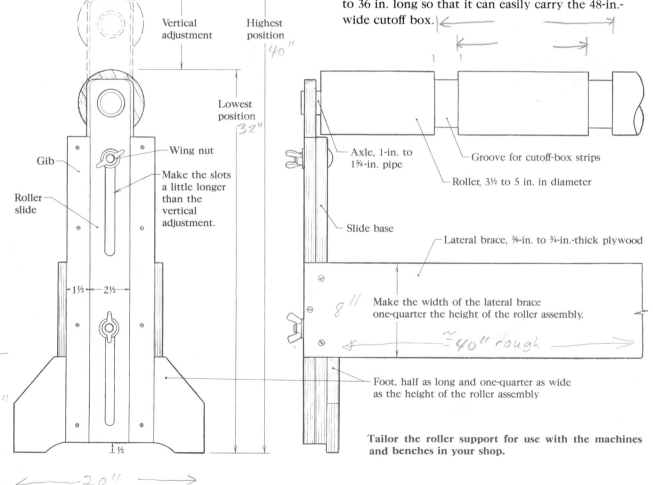

Side View

Vertical adjustment

Highest position

40"

Lowest position

32"

Gib

Wing nut

Make the slots a little longer than the vertical adjustment.

Roller slide

1½ 2½

1½

20"

Axle, 1-in. to 1¾-in. pipe

Groove for cutoff-box strips

Roller, 3½ to 5 in. in diameter

Slide base

Lateral brace, ⅜-in. to ¾-in.-thick plywood

8"

Make the width of the lateral brace one-quarter the height of the roller assembly.

40" rough

Foot, half as long and one-quarter as wide as the height of the roller assembly

Tailor the roller support for use with the machines and benches in your shop.

The roller—Once you've decided on the dimensions, make the roller. It should be 3½ in. to 5 in. in diameter. Glue thin pieces (about ¾ in. thick) face to face to get the required thickness. (A glued-up roller will also be more stable than one made of a single thick board.) You can turn one on a lathe, or use a tablesaw and a hand plane. Either way, make the diameter of the roller uniform from end to end. A tapered, cone-shaped roller will lead the stock sideways.

I'll describe how to make a roller using the tablesaw and a hand plane. To make hand-planing easier, choose stock that is straight-grained and relatively easy to work. Pine, Douglas fir, and Philippine mahogany all can be worked easily with hand tools.

1. Start by carefully jointing or hand-planing two adjoining surfaces of the roller blank straight and square to one another. Then rip the blank to a square the same width as the diameter you want, and cut the blank to the length of the roller. Find the exact center on each end by drawing diagonals and marking their point of intersection. Now draw circles of the correct diameter on the ends.

2. Tilt the sawblade to 45° and set the fence to rip on a tangent to the circle. Saw off one corner, rotate the blank and saw off another, keeping a square corner between the fence and saw table. A previously cut corner will be between the table and the fence for the last cut. This will make the piece a little less stable on the saw, so take extra care to prevent the blank from rotating as you feed it through the saw.

3. Tilt the saw to 67½° and repeat the above procedure to make a 16-sided blank. Keep a wide surface on the saw table until the last cut.

4. I use two pieces of pipe or dowel for the roller axles. The axle diameter shouldn't exceed 1¾ in. (Before you choose, make sure you have the bits to drill the holes in the roller and slides.) The axles fit into a hole drilled several inches into the center of each end of the roller—they should protrude about 2 in. Glue wooden axles in place or pin metal axles from the side.

Now set the roller aside and make the stand, which will hold the roller while you plane off the corners with a hand plane.

The stand—The stand consists of two legs connected by lateral braces. Each leg consists of a roller slide, which supports the roller and moves between two gibs fastened to a slide base. Carriage bolts with wing nuts fit through slots in the roller slide and a hole in the slide base, and fix the roller at the correct height. A foot is fixed to the slide base.

1. The slide bases, roller slides and gibs are made from four pieces of relatively straight, ¾-in. hardwood plywood or solid wood. Cut them as long as the height of the lowest surface with which the roller support will be used. Joint one edge of each piece straight and then rip the pieces 6 in. wide. Mark the straightened edge.

2. The slide bases are made from two pieces, the gibs and roller slides from the other two. Mark the faces as shown in the drawing on the opposite page. Tilt the saw 75° to the table and rip a gib off each of the two pieces, jointed edge against the fence. Then rip a support from each, placing the newly beveled edge against the fence. The remaining pieces make the other gibs, but don't rip them to width now.

3. Glue and nail or screw the first gib (with the straightened and marked edge) to the slide base, aligning their straightened edges. Do the same to the other leg.

4. Put the roller slide and the second gib in place on each slide base. To ensure easy movement of the slide, slip a shim of brown wrapping paper or two thicknesses of notebook paper between it and the first gib. Fasten the second gib in place. The edges of the second gib and the slide base will not be even; rip the assembly so the gibs are of equal width.

5. Next, lay out the vertical-adjustment slots on the roller slides near the top and bottom end. The slots

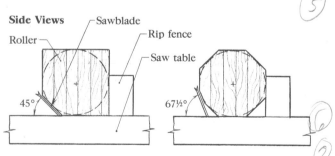

Side Views

Sawblade
Roller
Rip fence
Saw table
45°
67½°

To make the roller on the table, cut off the corners of the squared-up blank at 45° to make an octagon. Then set the blade at 67½° and make the blank 16-sided.

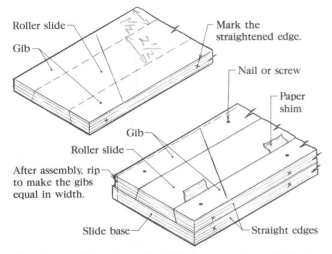

Cut the two gibs and a roller slide from one piece. Mark the face so the parts can be mounted together on the same slide base.

should be about 1½ in. longer than the required vertical adjustment and 1/16 in. wider than the diameter of the carriage bolts. Rout the slots using the shaper table, or drill a series of holes to clear the waste and file out the excess wood.

6. Drill holes in the top ends of the roller slides for the axles, positioning them so that material riding the roller clears the ends of the slides by about ½ in. I drill these holes the same diameter as the axles, then file or sand a little clearance into them. A bit of paraffin will help the axles turn easily.

7. Place the roller in one slide and put the slide between its gibs. Position the roller just above the slide base, and drill a hole for the carriage bolt through the slide base at the top of each slot. With the roller slide, slide base and roller in position, measure from the top of the roller and mark the height of the lowest position, minus 1 in., on the assembled leg. Remove the roller, leaving the support in place. Cut the support, gibs and slide base to length at the mark.

The Stand

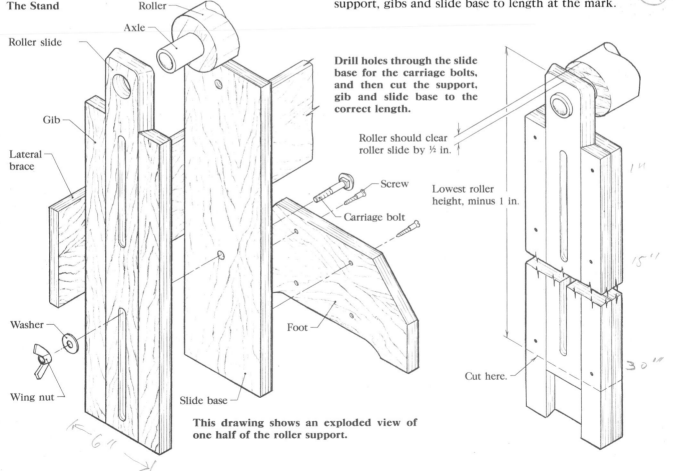

Drill holes through the slide base for the carriage bolts, and then cut the support, gib and slide base to the correct length.

This drawing shows an exploded view of one half of the roller support.

8. Feet for the roller support can be made from ½-in. or ¾-in. plywood or ¾-in. (or thicker) solid wood. Straighten the bottom edges on the jointer if necessary and rip the feet to width. Then trim one end and cut the feet to length.

9. The feet are more stable if they straddle irregularities in the floor, so I cut recesses in their bottom edges with a router or bandsaw.

10. The lateral braces keep the stand from racking, and hold the two legs apart at the proper distance so that the roller will run freely. Rip these braces to width. Find the length of the braces by adding the roller length (without axles), the thickness of both roller slides and ¼ in. for clearance. Trim and cut the lateral braces to this length.

Assembly

1. Assemble the stand with glue and screws. Attach the slide bases to the feet at right angles. Then attach the lateral braces to the legs, making sure that the assembly is square and that it stands perpendicular to the floor.

2. Put the roller in its slides and slide them into place. Fix the roller slides with carriage bolts, washers and wing nuts so that the roller is parallel to the floor. To adjust height, lay a straightedge on the saw table. Position it over one end of the roller, and adjust the slide. Then move the straightedge over the other end of the roller, and adjust that slide.

3. If you've roughed-out the roller on the tablesaw, plane the remaining corners off to make it round, using the stand to support it while planing. Here's how to keep the roller from spinning while you're planing it. Tie a long loop of rope (it should nearly touch the floor) around the roller. Place a board through the loop and stand with one foot on the board. Plane the roller with long strokes. When the roller is nearly round, turn the roller against a piece of chalk resting on the surface of a bench or machine. The chalk will mark the high points that need more planing.

4. The roller support and cutoff box are often used together, so you'll need to cut grooves in the roller to accommodate the guide strips on the bottom of the cutoff box. The grooves should be approximately twice as wide as the guide strips and slightly deeper than the guide-strip thickness. The roller should be centered under the cutoff box.

You can cut the grooves on the lathe or the tablesaw. To use the saw, raise the blade to the depth of the groove. Clamp a straightedge across the saw table so that a diameter of the blade and a diameter of the roller would form a straight line together. Carefully lower the roller on the moving sawblade and rotate it against the saw's rotation. Make several cuts and clean out the waste between them with a chisel.

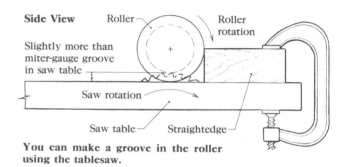

You can make a groove in the roller using the tablesaw.

Cutoff Box

The miter gauge on a tablesaw, which is used to cut the end of a board square to its edge, commonly has two serious drawbacks. First, its fence is too short to handle long pieces. Though the fence can be lengthened by attaching a board to its face, no advantage is gained if the board isn't absolutely straight and rigid.

Second, there are limits to the width of material that can be crosscut using the miter gauge. If the miter gauge is drawn back too far, not enough of its guiding bar will remain in the slot to ensure stability and accuracy.

A cutoff box solves these problems. It consists of a plywood base with two straight, wooden bars on top, and guide strips on the bottom that fit the grooves machined in the saw table. I also recommend that you fit a plastic chip guard over the box and a blade guard behind the push bar.

The material to be cut is placed in the box and the whole assembly is pushed across the saw. The push bar provides a much longer bearing surface than the fence of a miter gauge, and with about 54 in. between the two bars, you can crosscut full sheets of plywood—a necessary task in cabinet work. (If the cutoff box is not going to be used for cabinets, a 31-in. inside measurement might be adequate.)

A cutoff box, like any fine tool, isn't much good if it's inaccurate. Take care in constructing yours. The time will be well spent, because a cutoff box will help you to do accurate work quickly.

The base

1. Select a piece of ½-in. plywood without much warp or twist for the base. The grade isn't important, but it should have at least five plies. To determine the length of the base, you have to find out how far forward the box will need to travel to complete the cut when the blade is at its lowest and highest positions. These measurements determine how far the base must extend behind the face of the push bar.

To measure, draw a centerline across the largest blade the tablesaw will accommodate. Mount the blade and raise it approximately ½ in. above the table. (This will position the blade just above the base of the cutoff box.) Place the centerline at a right angle to the saw table, and then mark the table next to this line.

2. Now raise the blade as high as it will go. Mark the table next to the centerline. (The two marks may not be in the same place.) Also mark the table about

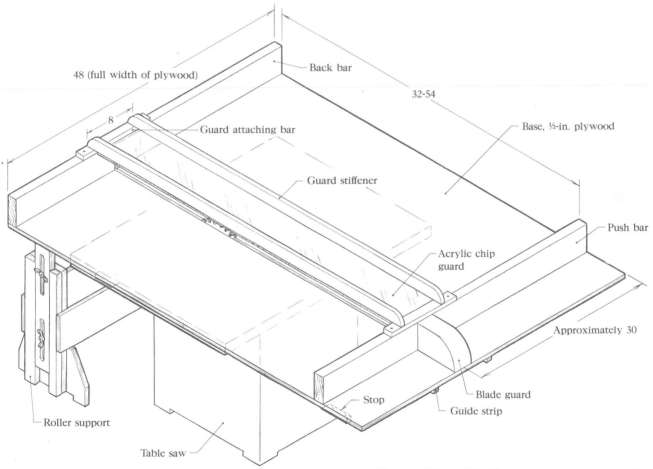

48 (full width of plywood)

Back bar

32-54

8

Guard attaching bar

Base, ½-in. plywood

Guard stiffener

Push bar

Acrylic chip guard

Approximately 30

Roller support

Stop

Blade guard

Guide strip

Table saw

The cutoff box slides in the miter-gauge grooves in the surface of most tablesaws. The acrylic chip guard is screwed to the bottom edge of the stiffeners.

2 in. in front of where the sawblade reenters the table, as shown in the drawing below. This line indicates the position of the blade guard when the inside
face of the push bar reaches the center of the blade.
Measure the distance between this line and the
centerline furthest from it (distance A in the drawing). The base should extend behind the face of the
push bar by at least this measurement.

   3. You can now determine the length of the cutoff-
box base by adding distance A, the thickness of the
back bar, and the distance that you want between
the two bars. Cut the plywood to length, leaving it a
full 48 in. wide.

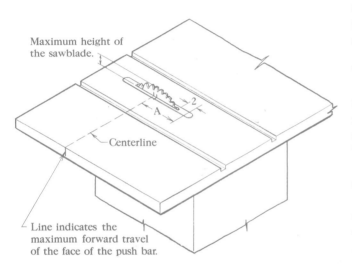

The base of the cutoff box must extend behind the face of
the push bar by the distance A.

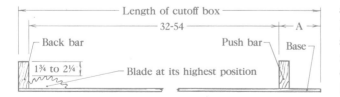

This side view of the cutoff box shows the dimensions de-
termining the length of the base.

The guide strips

1. Guide strips should be resistant to wear and relatively easy to machine and hand-plane. Straight-
grained walnut or oak will work well. Make the two
strips from one piece that is as long as the base and
wide enough to machine safely (at least 3 in. or 4 in.
wide). Avoid an extremely bowed or bent piece,
though one with a gentle, uniform bow is acceptable.

   2. Size the thickness of the piece so that it fits the
width of the groove with no slop, planing with a
hand plane or thickness planer, or ripping it on the
tablesaw. Joint one edge straight and rip the strips off.
They must not be wider than the groove is deep,
though they may be 1/32 in. or so narrower than this
depth. Make the strips about 1 in. shorter than the
total length of the box. When the box is put on end
on the floor, the strips won't be knocked loose.

The back bar

1. The back bar keeps the back edge of the cutoff
box straight and helps to hold the box together. It
must be at least 2 in. wider than the maximum height
of the blade. (A piece of 2x6 will make an adequate
back bar for most tablesaws.)

   Cut the 2x6 to a length of 48 in., joint one edge
straight and rip the piece to the finish width plus 1/4
in. (Boards will sometimes twist or warp after some
of the wood has been removed. The movement is
caused by tensions in the wood created during
growth or drying. Ripping the back bar slightly over
its final width allows for this movement before the
final straightening is done.)

   2. Joint one of the edges and check its straightness.
(This edge will be attached to the base.) Lay the bar
face down on a piece of plywood and draw a line
along the newly jointed edge with a sharp pencil.
Flop the bar over onto its other face, on the other
side of the line. If the jointed edge lines up with the
mark, the edge is straight. If there is a gap, joint and
check the edge again, drawing a new line. It is very
important to reduce the gap to less than 1/64 in.

The push bar

1. This bar is the most important part of the cutoff
box. The accuracy of the cut relies on the straightness of its face and the edge attached to the base.
The push bar should be made of wood that is rela-

tively easy to work and somewhat durable. Pine is too soft if the cutoff box is going to be used in a production shop, but it's satisfactory for the home shop. Douglas fir or Philippine mahogany are good choices.

Rough-cut the stock to the approximate length, joint one edge straight and rip to the finish width plus ¼ in. Joint one face straight and free of twist. Check for twist by laying a 12-in.-long straightedge on each end of the face. (Two combination-square blades work well.) Sight across the top edges of the two. If they're not parallel, the board is twisted and requires further jointing or planing.

2. Next, joint one edge straight and square to the straightened face. Check the edge and face for straightness as on the back bar. (You may have to finish the job with a hand plane because the jointer doesn't always leave a satisfactory surface. I can't overemphasize how important it is that both edge and face be straight. Don't be satisfied until any visible error is corrected.) Rip to width plus ¹⁄₁₆ in. Joint to width, then trim and cut to length.

Assembly

1. Before assembling the cutoff box, you must decide its position on the saw table. Both edges should overhang the table, and it is usually desirable to have more of the box on the right side of the saw kerf than on the left side. A 1½-in. overhang on the left side will allow you to fasten stops on both sides of the box and table, to keep the box from sliding too far forward. (If you haven't done so already, groove the roller support to take the cutoff-box guide strips.)

Lay the base on the saw table so the overhangs are correct. On the base, mark the position of one of the table's milled grooves. Turn the base over and clamp a straightedge (the push bar will do) at the mark, parallel to the plywood edge. Now lay the guide strip against the straightedge and fasten it with glue and brads or screws.

2. Lay the second guide strip in the table's other groove. If it is thinner than the groove is deep, shim it up flush with or slightly above the surface of the table (about ¹⁄₆₄ in.).

3. Apply glue to the guide strip, then place the base on the saw, inserting the first guide strip in its groove on the table. This will align the two guide strips. Nail through the base into the second guide

strip (keep moving the assembly so that you are always nailing over the saw table). If the guide strips are less than ⅜ in. thick, turn the base over and nail or screw through the second strip into the base. After the glue has had time to set, check that the base slides freely on the table. If it's tight, locate where it binds and scrape the guide with a cabinet scraper or chisel to get a smooth slide. A little paraffin will help.

4. Attach the back bar to the base with glue and screws. Be careful not to get a screw where the saw kerf will be.

5. Before attaching the push bar, you first need to cut the saw kerf in the box. Measure and mark distance A (determined when deciding the size of the base) in from the front end of the base. With a sharp saw, set approximately ¾ in. above the table and running, slide the box forward until the sawblade reaches the mark. Remember to set up the roller support to hold the cutoff box as it comes off the back of the saw table.

6. Position the inside face of the push bar where the kerf ends, and at a right angle to the kerf. Attach the bar to the base with a 1¾-in. screw near the edge with the smallest overhang—don't use glue. Clamp the other end to the base, and check that it is still at a right angle to the kerf. Place the clamp so that the cutoff box can slide freely.

7. The accuracy of the cutoff box depends on the push bar being straight and placed exactly 90° to the guide strips. The angle of the push bar to the guide strips is difficult to test by measuring, so I test it using a wide piece of plywood. (The wider the plywood, the more noticeable any inaccuracy in the angle will be, and the easier it will be for you to correct.) First, trim one end of the plywood. Keep in mind that because the push bar is fastened only at its ends, pushing on its center may cause it to bow. Push on the plywood base instead of the push bar, or have an assistant pull the box through by its back bar.

8. Next, flop the test piece over (index against the same edge), and cut a short strip (about ¾ in. to 1 in.) off the end you just trimmed. Measure the length of the strip (the lesser dimension, along the grain) at each edge. The difference in the two measurements will be double the error in the position of the push bar. For example, a difference of ⅛ in. indicates that the push bar is deflected ¹⁄₁₆ in. from perpendicular to

the guide strips. Adjust the push bar at the clamped end until there is no more than a ¼-in. difference on a 48-in.-wide test strip. It is not uncommon, and is very desirable, to get the difference down to .005 in. (which is measurable only with a micrometer).

9. When you've achieved the proper tolerance, place a piece of plywood that is at least 4 in. wide against the front of the push bar, and tack it to the base to act as a temporary fence. With the push bar still clamped in place, drill and countersink clearance holes through the base and pilot holes into the push bar for 1¾-in. flathead screws.

10. These next steps should be done quickly so that you can test the position of the push bar again before the glue sets. Remove the push bar, apply glue to its bottom edge, replace it against the plywood fence and secure it with screws. Check the position by cutting another test strip. If you find that adjustments are necessary, remove the screws and the push bar. Clean up the glue, and then start over with step 6. You will have to shift the push bar forward about ⅜ in. or drill new screw holes to prevent the screws from pulling into their original holes, which would shift the push bar.

The chip guard—A chip guard, shown in the drawing on p. 113, will protect the operator from flying chips, dust and splinters. The stiffeners and attaching bars should be made of a strong wood such as oak. The guard is high-impact acrylic plastic, 3⁄16 in. or ¼ in. thick. Cut the plastic to size on the tablesaw. If it doesn't saw cleanly, cut it oversized and joint it to final dimensions with the router. Center the chip-guard assembly over the kerf in the cutoff box and attach it with screws, but no glue. If the acrylic has to be replaced, you'll need to be able to remove it.

Stops—Stops attached to the underside of the cutoff-box base and the edges of the saw table keep the cutoff box from being pushed completely off the saw and roller. You can use two pairs, one for each edge of the saw table. Good stops can be made from pieces of steel bar stock, ½ in. square. The stops should be made in pairs, so the ends mate. The angles on the ends reduce the chance of the box jumping over the stop. Attach the stops securely to prevent them from breaking loose. Make sure there is clearance for the

stop to pass between the top of the table and the top of the saw's rip-fence rail, bar or tube. If there is no satisfactory mounting surface on the edge of the saw table, you can provide a surface by bolting a piece of angle iron or channel iron to the table.

1. Lay out the stops on a single, long piece of bar stock. Drill and tap the holes before cutting off the individual pieces—it's easier to hold longer pieces secure. Because many saws have limited clearance between the saw table and the rip-fence rail, leaving no room for nuts, it's usually necessary to drill and tap the base part of the stop and pass the bolts down through the base. You may also have to tap the holes in the edges of the saw table.

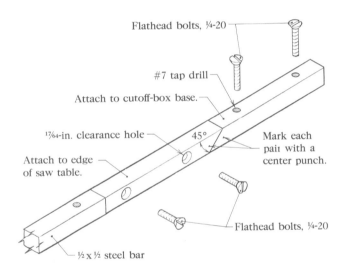

Make the stops in pairs, each pair 5 in. to 8 in. long.

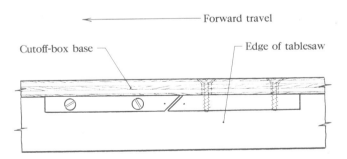

The stop attached to the cutoff-box base engages the stop attached to the edge of the saw table.

2. Before cutting the pieces apart with a hacksaw, mark them with a center punch so they can be kept in matched sets. That way, an irregular cut on the mating surfaces will not matter. Chamfer the sharp edges and corners with a file.

3. To position the stops, put the cutoff box on the saw, and advance it until the inside face of the push bar is about ⅛ in. beyond the point of maximum forward travel, as shown in the drawing below. Locate the stops so that the braces or casting webs on the underside of the saw table won't interfere with the bolts. Drill the tap or clearance holes through the edge of the saw table, and then fasten the table-half of each stop in place.

4. Next position the stops on the cutoff-box base. The stops on both sides of the table should engage at the same time and should be clear of the edge of the saw table so that the box can move freely. Drill and countersink the clearance holes in the base, and then bolt the base-half of each stop in place.

Blade guard

1. To further protect the saw operator, I strongly recommend that you add a blade guard to cover the sawblade where it exits the push bar. To do this, you first need to determine the size of the guard by raising the sawblade to its maximum height and advancing the cutoff box to the stops.

2. Make the guard from stock about 2¼ in. thick, or glue up stock to this thickness. Joint an edge (use a piece long enough to be safe on the jointer), and rip to width. Trim one end square on the cutoff box. Make sure that this end and the jointed edge fit into the corner formed by the base and the outside face of the push bar, then cut the piece to length.

3. Raise the blade and push the cutoff box forward to the stops. Place the guard blank in position beside the blade and mark out the blade's profile on the blank to help determine where the blade guard should be cut. Cut out the guard on the bandsaw or cutoff box as shown in the drawing below.

4. Glue the guard in place, and the cutoff box is complete. It should be an accurate and helpful fixture for many years.

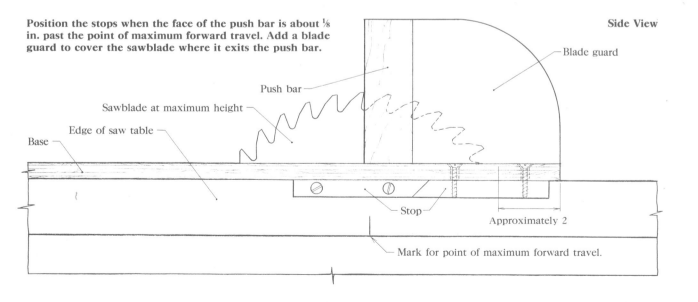

Position the stops when the face of the push bar is about ⅛ in. past the point of maximum forward travel. Add a blade guard to cover the sawblade where it exits the push bar.

Side View

Blade guard

Push bar

Sawblade at maximum height

Edge of saw table

Base

Stop

Approximately 2

Mark for point of maximum forward travel.

Miter Cutoff Box

Good-fitting miters look nice and are fairly strong, but cutting them can be difficult. The tablesaw miter gauge is difficult to keep adjusted accurately, and any error in the setup for a mitered frame is multiplied eight times. I prefer a miter cutoff box. This one will cut miters in wood up to 3 in. wide. The box is made exactly like the cutoff box except that a recess is cut in the back bar to accommodate long stock, and miter push bars are added.

Attaching the miter push bar to the base at exactly 45° to the kerf can be difficult. I attach each miter push bar with one screw through the base near the kerf and I clamp the other end with a temporary clamp, as shown in the drawing below. This way, you can make test cuts and adjust the bars perfectly before fixing them permanently.

To test the accuracy of one of the push bars, miter a piece of scrap wood about 3 in. wide. (The scrap must have parallel edges.) Position the two halves to form a 90° angle. Adjust the push bar if the angle is off; anchor it with a second screw through the base.

To set the second push bar, miter four pieces of 3-in.-wide stock to make a small frame. In order to keep the same face of the stock up for all the cuts, you must use one bar for four of the cuts and the other bar for the other four. Assemble the frame on a tabletop. If it has four tight joints, the second bar is in the correct position—lock it in place with a second screw. If the joints aren't tight, adjust the second bar and test it again. (Don't be satisfied until it's perfect.)

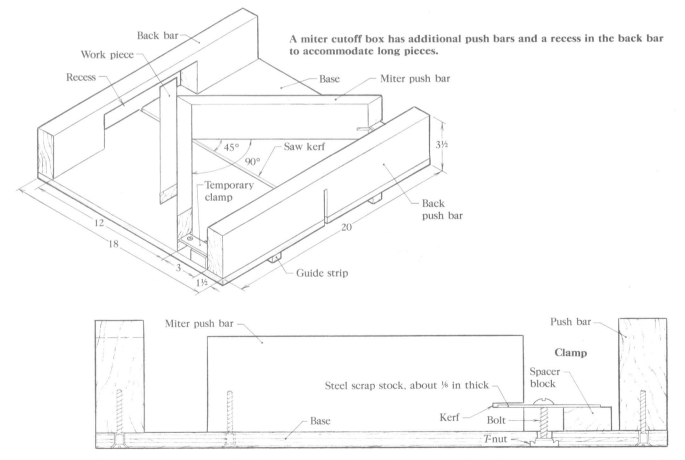

A miter cutoff box has additional push bars and a recess in the back bar to accommodate long pieces.

This clamp allows you to adjust the setting of the miter push bars. After final adjustments are made, anchor each miter push bar with one or two more screws.

Edge-Band Trimmer

A solid-wood band applied to a plywood edge hides ugly end grain and holds screws well. It is usually easier to make banding slightly oversized, glue it to the plywood edge, and then trim it flush with the faces of the plywood.

You can plane the banding flush or use an edge-band trimmer. The trimmer is just a homemade router subbase that keeps the bit level with the plywood surface and guides it along the banding. The trimmer is especially useful when bandings have twisted grain that a plane iron might dig into.

Use a piece of hardwood plywood or particleboard for the trimmer base. Though the dimensions given are not critical, increasing the size of the base by much will decrease its accuracy. A large base tends to bridge over concave plywood, which leaves the

trimmed band higher than the plywood face. Use solid wood for the fence.

The plastic subbase that comes with the router is attached with short bolts. You'll need longer bolts to attach the router to the plywood trimmer base, and a couple of ¼-in. by 2-in. carriage bolts, washers and wing nuts to attach the fence to the base.

Construction

1. Saw and joint the trimmer base and fence to size. Remove the plastic router subbase and fasten the router in the center of the length of the trimmer base and almost flush with one edge. (Counterdrill the holes for the screws about ¼ in. deep into the bottom of the base.) Plunge through the trimmer base with a ¾-in. router bit to make a bit-clearance hole. If you drill this hole, be sure that you center it over the router base.

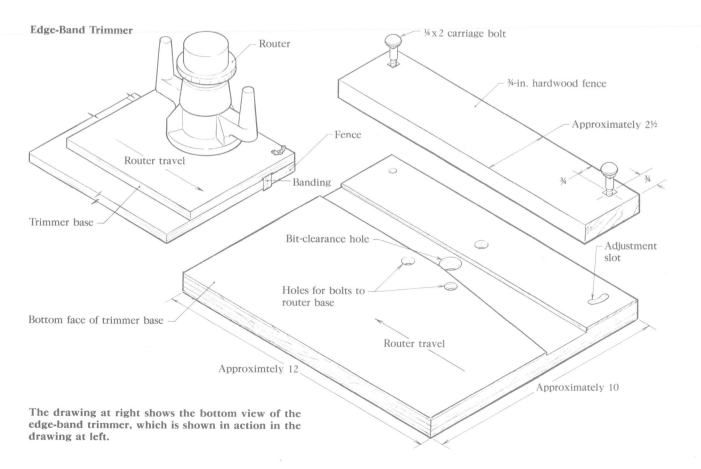

Edge-Band Trimmer

Router

Router travel

Fence

Banding

Trimmer base

Bottom face of trimmer base

Approximtely 12

¼ x 2 carriage bolt

¾-in. hardwood fence

Approximately 2½

¾   ¾

Bit-clearance hole

Holes for bolts to router base

Adjustment slot

Router travel

Approximately 10

The drawing at right shows the bottom view of the edge-band trimmer, which is shown in action in the drawing at left.

2. Drill holes in each end of the fence for the carriage bolts with a bit the same size as the carriage bolt. Clamp the fence to the wooden base, on a tangent to the bit-clearance hole and parallel to the edge of the wooden base, as shown in the drawing below. Drill through the base, centering the bit in the bolt holes in the fence. Drop a bolt through one hole (A) and pivot the fence so it just covers the bit-clearance hole. Clamp the fence in this position and drill through the other hole (B).

3. Join the two B holes in the base with a curved slot. (If the pivot and slot are reversed, the trimmer will have to be fed against the band in the wrong direction.) Drill a series of holes and file out the waste. Position the drill bit for the holes by pivoting the guide from one of the B holes to the other.

To rout the slot on the shaper table, use a bit $\frac{1}{16}$ in. larger than the bolt diameter. Fix a dowel near one edge of a piece of scrap plywood, larger than the trimmer base. Place the base hole (A) on the dowel and one of the B holes over the router bit, then clamp the scrap to the table. Pivot the base on the dowel to clear the waste between the two B holes.

4. Rout the groove on the bottom of the base (as shown on p. 119). Rout it about $\frac{1}{4}$ in. wider than the clearance hole and about $\frac{1}{8}$ in. deep. Pivot the fence, as shown below at left, to draw the line of the flare. Rout the flare freehand or against a fence.

5. Chuck a $\frac{3}{4}$-in. straight bit in the router and mount it on the trimmer. Adjust the fence so enough bit is showing to trim the banding thickness. The bit should be flush with the base bottom.

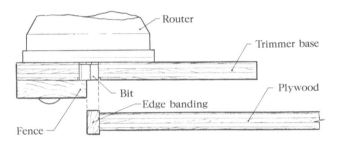

To use the trimmer, the bit should be flush with the bottom of the base and extend beyond the fence by the thickness of the banding, or a little more.

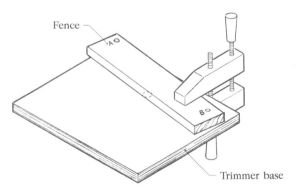

Clamp the fence on a tangent to the bit-clearance hole and parallel to the edge of the base. Drill holes at A and B.

Pivot the fence so that it just covers the hole and then drill another hole at B.

Move the router so that the bit cuts into, rather than out of, the banding (as shown in the drawing on p. 119). This will help keep the bit from snagging and tearing the grain. If you tip the trimmer, it will cut too deeply into the banding. Avoid tipping by keeping a constant pressure on the part of the trimmer base that slides on the plywood. Sand lightly after routing to finish the job off nicely.

6. The trimmer also works well for trimming wood banding on panels covered with plastic laminate. Use the setup described above, but adjust the fence to leave a thin sliver of untrimmed banding at the glue line. This keeps the bit from touching the laminate and cutting through its very thin layer of color. After routing, trim this sliver with a chisel.

Router-Bit Gauges

The router is an excellent tool for making dado and rabbet joints. Its bit cuts at high speed and cleanly, and unlike a tablesaw, a router can cut a dado or rabbet of uniform depth in a warped board, because its small base will follow the contours of the board.

The major disadvantage of using the router for this work is that the setup can be a little difficult. You often have to guide the router by pushing its subbase along a straightedge. The straightedge must be clamped to the board parallel to the position of the dado or rabbet. It should be positioned the distance from the edge of the subbase to either cutting edge of the router bit. (The distance will vary, depending on the diameter of the router bit you are using.) With a bit gauge, you can position the straightedge accurately and quickly. The width of each gauge matches the distance from the edge of the subbase to either the near or far side of the router bit.

To make the bit gauges, first make a simple jig with a fence by nailing a straight piece of ½-in. or ¾-in.-thick wood to a plywood base. (Scrap will do.) The bit gauge can be made of thin plywood, Masonite or plastic, but must have a straight edge. Fasten the bit-gauge blank to the base so its straight edge is tight against the fence. Keep the brads or screws close to the fence, out of the bit's path, and set them below the surface, out of the way of the router subbase. Chuck the bit in the router and set it deep enough to cut just through the blank, and run the router against the fence, as shown in the drawing below. For an inside gauge, cut the whole length of the blank. For an outside gauge, cut a few inches into the blank. A finished pair of gauges will look like the ones below. Mark all pairs for easy identification.

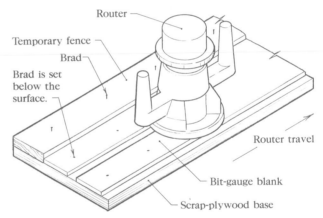

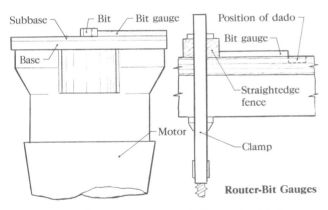

Use a router-bit gauge to set up dadoes and rabbets accurately and quickly.

Make the gauges for each bit using a temporary jig. Fasten the bit-gauge blank with a screw or brad so its straight edge is against the fence. Slide the edge of the router subbase along the fence and rout through the blank.

You will need two gauges for each bit: one to gauge to the near side of the bit (I call this an inside gauge), one to gauge to the far side (an outside gauge). If your router base is round, but not exactly concentric to the bit, the distance between the bit and edge of the base will vary around the subbase. Make the guide for one particular spot on the circumference; always place that spot against the fence.

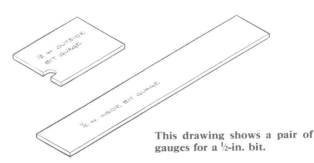

This drawing shows a pair of gauges for a ½-in. bit.

Router Shaper Table

A router can be guided across the work by a number of methods. When routing large boards, it's easy to move the router against a straightedge clamped to the board. Small fence attachments, handy for routing a short distance in from an edge or end, can be purchased for most routers. Some router bits have pilots that index against the edge of the board.

There are times, however, when it's not practical to use these methods—for example, when the board is too small to take a straightedge, or too awkward to hold securely while routing. The router shaper table will often solve these problems.

The shaper table, in its simplest form, is just a box that holds the router upside down so only its bit protrudes above the top of the box. Several built-in refinements can make the table easier and safer to use.

The top surface should be large enough to support the piece being worked. In cabinetmaking, the shaper table can be used to great advantage in drawer construction, which requires a top 18 in. by 26 in. A top that is a little larger may come in handy at times, but requires more storage space.

I recommend using ¾-in.-thick hardwood plywood for the top. For a more durable top, use plastic laminate glued to medium-density particleboard or fir plywood. (A plastic-laminate top also allows the work to slide easier.) Remember to apply the laminate to both surfaces to keep the top from warping.

A plate let into the top to hold the router base is a must. Without it, the heads of the bolts used to attach the router to the table would eventually pull through the top. A piece of ¼-in.-thick acrylic makes a good plate. (Aluminum, ³⁄₁₆ in. or ¼ in. thick, is okay, too.) The plate should extend 1 in. to 2 in. beyond the perimeter of the router base. (You must remove the subbase from the router base.)

The table's legs and feet should be made from ¾-in. plywood. If the legs are set 4 in. to 6 in. in from each end of the top, it will give the top an overhang for easy clamping. The table should be high enough for the router motor to be removed easily without lifting or tilting the table.

Router Shaper Table

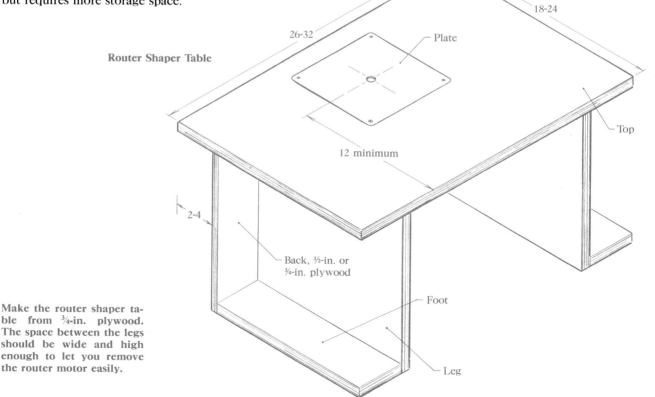

Make the router shaper table from ¾-in. plywood. The space between the legs should be wide and high enough to let you remove the router motor easily.

Make the back from ½-in. or ¾-in.-thick plywood. It should be as wide as the legs are long, and as long as the top. The back prevents the shaper table from racking and stiffens the top, keeping it from sagging.

Construction

1. Cut all the parts, including the acrylic plate, to size on the tablesaw using the rip fence and cutoff box. (If the acrylic doesn't saw very smoothly, you can joint it to size.) Metal plates will need to be cut with the appropriate metalworking tools. Round one corner of each foot if desired, then assemble the pieces with glue and nails or screws. Attach the feet to the legs, then the back to the feet and legs. If you are using plastic laminate on the top, glue it to both faces of the top now, but don't attach the top yet.

2. Lay out the position of the plate on the top. Center it on the length of the top and closer to the back edge than the front. Chuck a ¾-in. straight bit in the router and set it the same depth as the plate

thickness or a few thousandths of an inch deeper. (If the recess is too shallow, it will be difficult to make it deeper. If it is too deep, it can be shimmed to the correct depth.)

3. Use the ¾-in. bit gauge to locate a straightedge fence for the first cut along the back edge of the top. If there isn't room to clamp the straightedge in place, move to the other side of the cut and locate it with an outside bit gauge, as shown in the drawing below. (If you don't get a straight cut, move the straightedge toward the cut by the amount of the error and make another pass. Mistakes like this won't matter on the other three perimeter cuts because the fence is on the outside of the recess.)

4. Place the plate in position against the edge of the first cut and put the bit gauge against the end of the plate as shown in the drawing below. Clamp the straightedge in place, and mark where the cut should end. Remove the plate and rout as before, stopping at the mark.

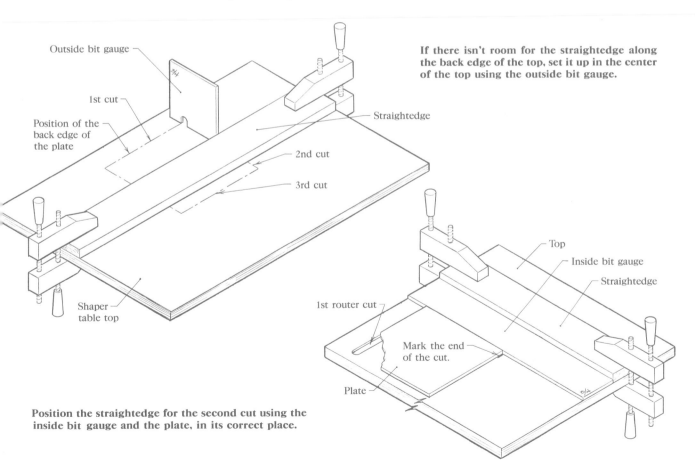

If there isn't room for the straightedge along the back edge of the top, set it up in the center of the top using the outside bit gauge.

Position the straightedge for the second cut using the inside bit gauge and the plate, in its correct place.

5. Chisel out the round corner left by the first two cuts, or round the corner of the plate to match the radius of the router bit. Lay the plate flush with the routed corner, set up the straightedge with the bit gauge, and rout the third side as before. Then do the same for the last perimeter cut.

6. Rout out the waste between the perimeter cuts freehand. Be sure to start along one edge and work back and forth toward the opposite edge. If you work from the outside toward the center, as when mowing a lawn, you will have cut away the router's support when you reach the center.

7. Rout or saw a hole approximately in the center of the recess for the router base to pass through. The hole should be slightly larger than the base, but it shouldn't be a tight fit. Put the plate in the recess, position the router base on the underside, and mark the bolt holes for attaching it to the plate. Make sure the clamp that tightens the router motor into the base is easily accessible.

8. Leave the plate in the recess and mark the holes for the flathead stove bolts that secure it to the top. Drill the holes in the plate (countersink those on the top). Attach the plate to the top of the shaper table, and the router base to the plate. Place the top on the legs. If you have a plastic-laminate top, you may wish to fasten it to the legs from the underside with cleats. Otherwise, screw down through the top into the legs. Countersink the screwheads so they won't scratch the work.

9. With a ¾-in. straight bit in the router, insert the motor in the router base and clamp it. Turn on the power, carefully hold the motor while loosening the clamp, and raise the bit up through the plate. (This will work for acrylic or aluminum, though you may want to make the hole in an aluminum plate on a drill press.)

10. The shaper table is now complete, but there are some further refinements you can make. Rather than clamp a straightedge to the table, you can add a

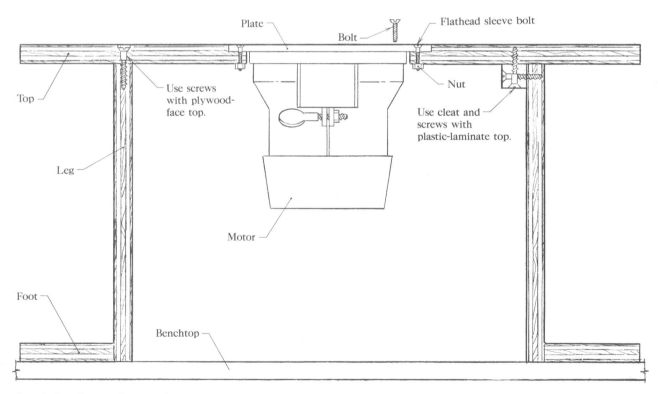

Attach the plate to the top, the router base to the plate and the top to the legs.

fence. Slot one end to allow for a pivoting adjustment, and attach it with carriage bolts and wing nuts. Drill a series of holes in the top so the fence may be moved across the table. Space the holes so the adjustments overlap.

You can add a door to the open side of the base to channel the shavings. You'll also need to add an external switch, a vacuum to suck out the shavings, and vent holes to prevent the motor from overheating. If some of the vent holes are made in the plate, cooling air will be drawn past the motor when the holes aren't covered by the piece being machined.

11. Always be sure to clamp the motor into the router base before turning it on. If you don't, the motor will spin out of the base, which could be dangerous. By adding a plunger switch that provides power to the on/off switch only when the door of the base is closed, you can eliminate some of the danger: the motor can't be turned on unless the door is closed and it won't be able to fall out of the confined space.

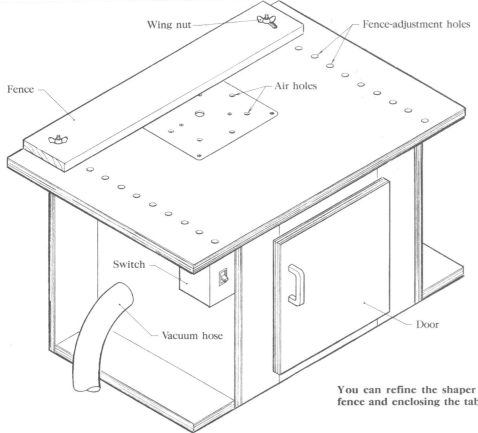

You can refine the shaper table by adding an adjustable fence and enclosing the table to collect dust.

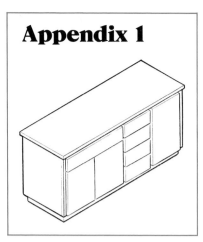

Appendix 1

Appliance Sizes

Whether an appliance is built into a cabinet or is freestanding, its size is crucial to cabinet layout and construction. The drawings in this appendix illustrate the range of dimensions for a variety of appliances. These drawings will be a helpful reference when planning your kitchen, but remember that the only way to be sure that you've got the correct measurements is to check the manufacturers' specification sheets. Don't risk an approximation.

When planning your kitchen, try to leave enough space for the largest size of a particular appliance, even though you may actually use the smallest one; this way, a new appliance can be installed later on without altering the cabinets. For appliances built into a cabinet, use wide face-frame stiles, which can be trimmed back if you get a larger appliance.

Here are a couple of tips to improve the looks of cabinets that are next to freestanding appliances, such as refrigerators and some ranges. If the cabinet is going to fit tightly against the appliance, make the countertop and toeboard flush with the hidden end, so there won't be a gap between the appliance and the cabinet. If the cabinet is going to fit loosely against the appliance, you'll see part of its end, so make sure you use face material, not softwood plywood, to make that end.

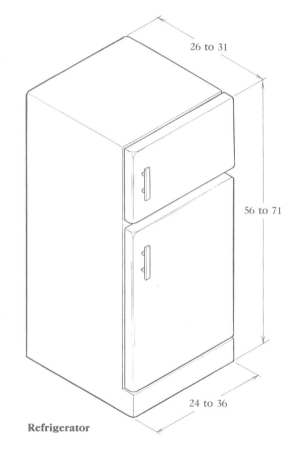

26 to 31

56 to 71

24 to 36

Refrigerator

Slide-In Range

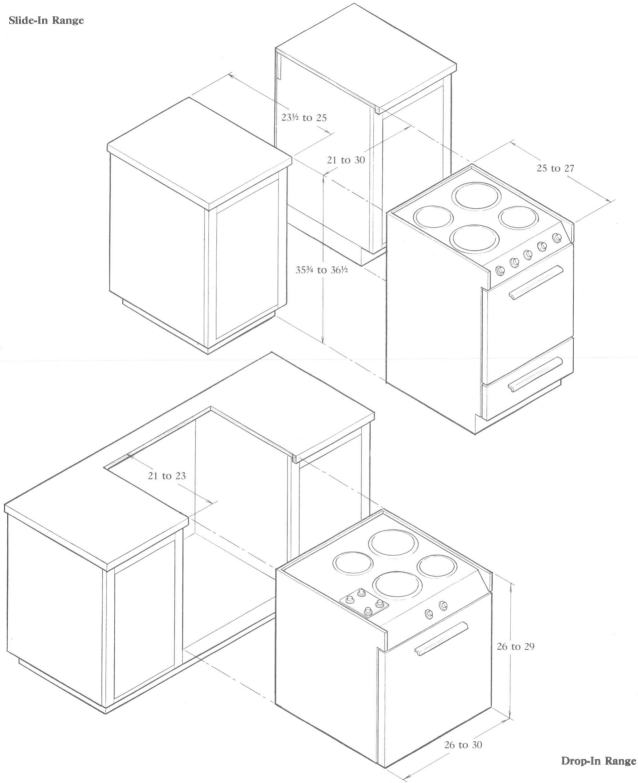

23½ to 25

21 to 30

25 to 27

35¾ to 36½

21 to 23

26 to 29

26 to 30

Drop-In Range

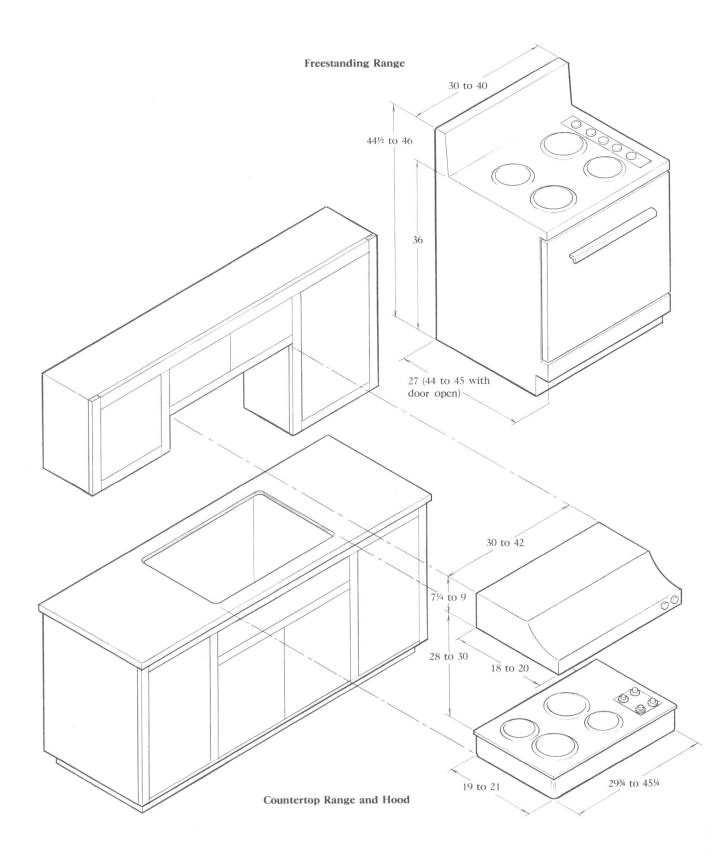

Freestanding Range

30 to 40

44½ to 46

36

27 (44 to 45 with door open)

30 to 42

7¼ to 9

28 to 30

18 to 20

19 to 21

29¾ to 45¼

Countertop Range and Hood

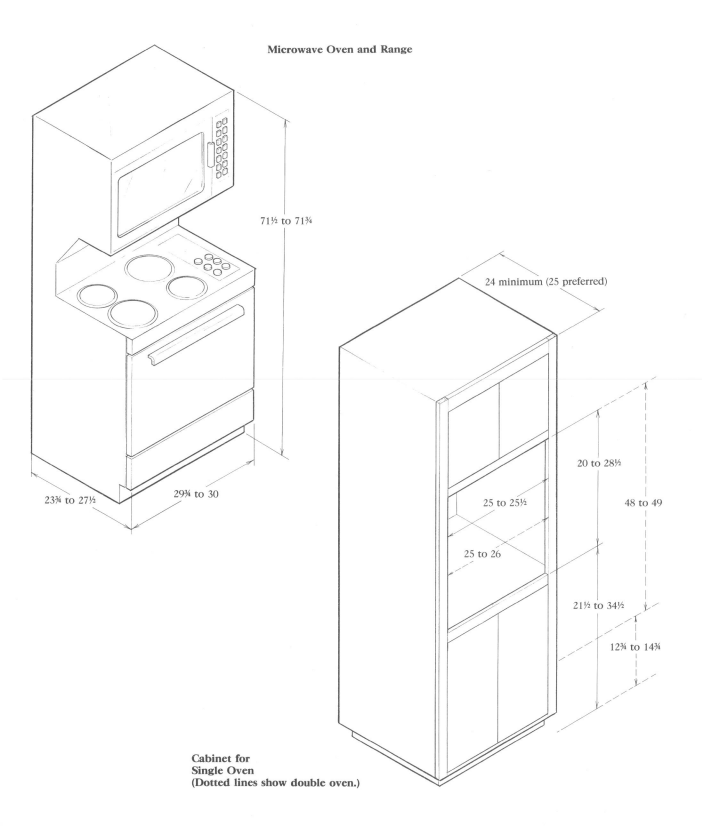

Microwave Oven and Range

71½ to 71¾

23¾ to 27½

29¾ to 30

24 minimum (25 preferred)

20 to 28½

48 to 49

25 to 25½

25 to 26

21½ to 34½

12¾ to 14¾

**Cabinet for
Single Oven
(Dotted lines show double oven.)**

Washer and Dryer

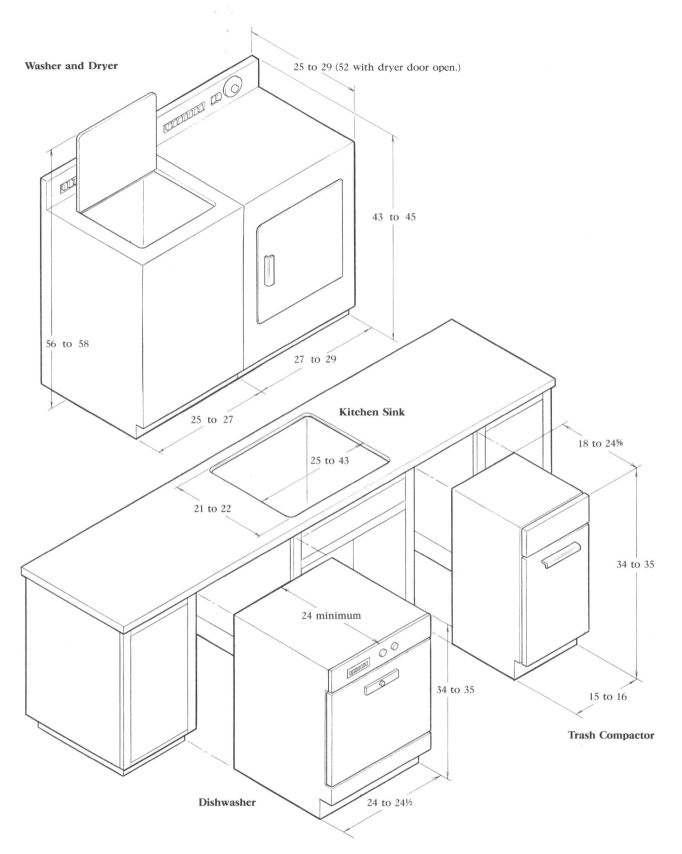

25 to 29 (52 with dryer door open.)

43 to 45

56 to 58

27 to 29

25 to 27

Kitchen Sink

25 to 43

21 to 22

18 to 24⅝

34 to 35

24 minimum

34 to 35

15 to 16

Trash Compactor

Dishwasher

24 to 24½

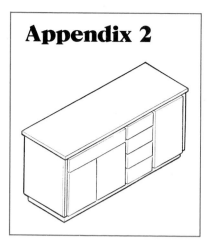

Appendix 2

Tools

The two lists in this appendix summarize useful tools for kitchen cabinetmaking. The first is a list of the necessary tools for beginners, the second is a list of tools that are nice to acquire as interest and budget allow. I offer these lists as guides; as you develop your skills, you'll probably find that you require specialized tools not listed here.

Beginner's List of Tools

Power tools—A tablesaw can be set up to handle all the cutting necessary for cabinet work. I recommend a 10-in., tilting-arbor tablesaw with a 1-HP, 220-volt motor. (Tablesaws are sized by the maximum blade diameter a model will take; for example, a 10-in. saw takes a blade no larger than 10 in. in diameter.) Never buy a tablesaw with a tilting table—in my opinion, they're unsafe. When buying a tablesaw, make sure that the rip fence locks down securely, parallel to the slots in the table.

A jointer will straighten the edge or face of a board. In kitchen cabinetmaking, a jointer is used mostly to machine face-frame parts. Jointers are sized by maximum blade length; I find a 4-in. jointer is adequate for my work, but bigger would be better. I also prefer to use jointers with adjustable outfeed tables (they all have adjustable infeed tables).

Before purchasing a jointer, make sure the infeed and outfeed tables are parallel. A surprising number of jointers on the market don't have parallel tables, and it's impossible to straighten material on them.

Here's a simple test to determine whether or not the tables are parallel. Lay a long level (or other straightedge) on the outfeed table. Raise or lower the infeed table until several strips of paper will just slip between it and the level. If the same number of paper strips fit at each end of the infeed table, the tables are perfectly parallel. A variation of two pieces of thin paper (about .006 in., if you're using typing paper) from one end to the other is acceptable.

A ⅞-HP router (or larger) with ¼-in., ½-in. and ¾-in. carbide-tipped straight bits is an invaluable tool. Some routers have a poorly machined collet (the sleeve that holds the bit shank), which can cause the bit to get stuck in the machine. When buying a router, look into the collet under good light to make sure it's bright and smooth. (A poorly machined collet has a series of rings or machine marks on its inside.)

You'll also need an electric drill. One with a ¼-in. chuck is satisfactory, but one with a ⅜-in. chuck and a variable-speed reversing motor (to use with a power screwdriver) is better. Get a selection of drill bits in ¹⁄₁₆-in. increments, from ⅛ in. to ⅜ in. in diameter.

Layout tools—An 8-ft. to 12-ft. tape measure, a framing square and a combination square are essential for layout. You will also need a 2-ft.-long level, and a scriber. (If you wish, you can substitute a compass for a scriber.)

Cutting and shaping tools—A 10-point to 12-point crosscut handsaw is necessary, as are ½-in., ¾-in. and 1-in. chisels. You'll also need a low-angle block plane; if you're going to buy a new one, buy the best that you can afford.

Assembly tools—A 16-oz., flat-face hammer is a must. You also should have ½₂-in. and ⅔₂-in. nail sets. For clamps, you will need pipe clamps, ¾ in. in diameter, in assorted lengths up to 8 ft. long, two hand-screw clamps with 6 in. between the jaws and two C-clamps that will take 3 in. between the jaws. Have a selection of screwdrivers available, too.

Miscellaneous tools—Be sure to have on hand a dowel jig, hacksaw, pliers, a putty knife, a 10-in. mill bastard file, and a 5-in. scraper. You will also need medium and fine sharpening stones (India or carborundum will do fine).

List of Nice-but-not-Necessary Tools

Power tools—A bandsaw is one of the most useful tools. Bandsaws are sized by the diameter of the wheels on which the blade runs—a 14-in. bandsaw is the smallest one you should consider. A portable jigsaw and orbital sander come in handy, too. To fill out your set of router bits, get a ¾-in. corebox bit, a ¼-in. quarter-round bit for bullnosing and a kit of trimmer bits for plastic laminate. I also recommend filling in your drill-bit set with the odd sizes, measured in thirty-seconds of an inch (³₃₂ in., ⁵₃₂ in., etc.) up to ¹⁵₃₂ in. Also try to get power-screwdriver bits and a No. 5 self-centering bit.

Layout tools—Get a sliding *T*-bevel, dividers and, if you'll be installing a lazy Susan, trammel points.

Cutting and shaping tools—You may need a dovetail saw (which is a small backsaw), a coping saw, and a 14-in. jack plane, as well as a bit brace and a set of auger bits.

Assembly tools—A brad pusher is nice to have on hand, and so are a rubber mallet and a bench vise. You can never have too many clamps: I recommend additional pipe clamps, two hand-screw clamps with 8 in. between the jaws and two 4-in. *C*-clamps.

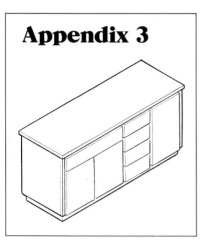

Appendix 3

Plan of Procedure for Kitchen Cabinetmaking

One of the hardest things about kitchen cabinetmaking is keeping track of all the necessary tasks and doing them in the right order. The lists below summarize the steps I go through in the four phases of building a set of cabinets. I take all the cabinets through each phase at once. (Refer to the chapters in parentheses for details on each step.)

Phase 1: The Basic Case

1. Rough-cut the parts of the case to length and width (Chapter 4).
2. Edge-band where necessary (Chapter 4).
3. Finish-cut the parts (Chapter 4).
4. Cut all the joints and the notches for the nail rail (Chapter 5).
5. Sand the parts (Chapter 6).
6. Secure drawer guides to dust panels (Chapter 10).
7. Install metal shelf standard for adjustable shelving (Chapter 7).
8. Assemble the case (Chapter 7).

Phase 2: The Face Frame

All this information appears in Chapter 8.
1. Select and rough-cut the parts.
2. Joint one edge of each part.
3. Rip the parts to width plus $\frac{1}{16}$ in.
4. Joint the parts to width.
5. Trim and cut them to length.
6. Drill for the dowels.
7. Assemble the frame.
8. Fasten the frame to the case.

Phase 3: Doors and Drawers

1. Make the faces (Chapter 9).
2. Make the drawers (Chapter 10).

Phase 4: Toeboards and Countertops

1. Rip the toeboard stock to width (Chapter 12).
2. Miter the ends where necessary (Chapter 12).
3. Trim and cut toeboard parts to length (Chapter 12).
4. Assemble (Chapter 12).
5. Rough-cut the underlayment (Chapter 13).
6. Attach the edge banding to the underlayment (Chapter 13).
7. Rip to finish width (Chapter 13).
8. Crosscut to finish length (Chapter 13).
9. Attach the underlayment to the case.
10. Install the countertop material (Chapter 14).

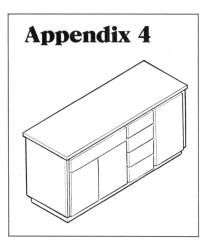

Appendix 4

Forms for the Estimate of Materials, Cutting List and Panel Layout

After filling out the estimate of materials form at right, use the form on p. 136 to prepare the cutting list. I usually work on one phase of construction at a time: the basic case first, the face frame second, doors and drawers third, and the toeboard and countertop last. I cut all the parts and complete each phase before moving on to fill out the list and cut materials for the next one.

Use the form on p. 137 to determine the best way to cut the sheets of plywood or particleboard. (You can also use these forms to estimate the amount of material necessary for the job.) The rectangles represent 48-in. by 96-in. panels, and each one is marked for multiple-cut sizes of 24 in. and 32 in. (p. 23). Check the appropriate blanks to indicate the panel thickness and type of material.

Estimate of Materials

Job _____ Unit _____ Date _____
Prepared by _____ Checked by _____

	No. of Parts	Name of Part	Thick.	Width	Length	Type of Material	Special Notes

Cutting List

Job _____   Unit _____   Date _____

Prepared by _____   **Checked by** _____

All dimensions are finish size unless otherwise specified.

	No. of Parts	Name of Part	Thick.	Width R F			Length R F			Type of Material	Special Notes

Form for Panel Layout

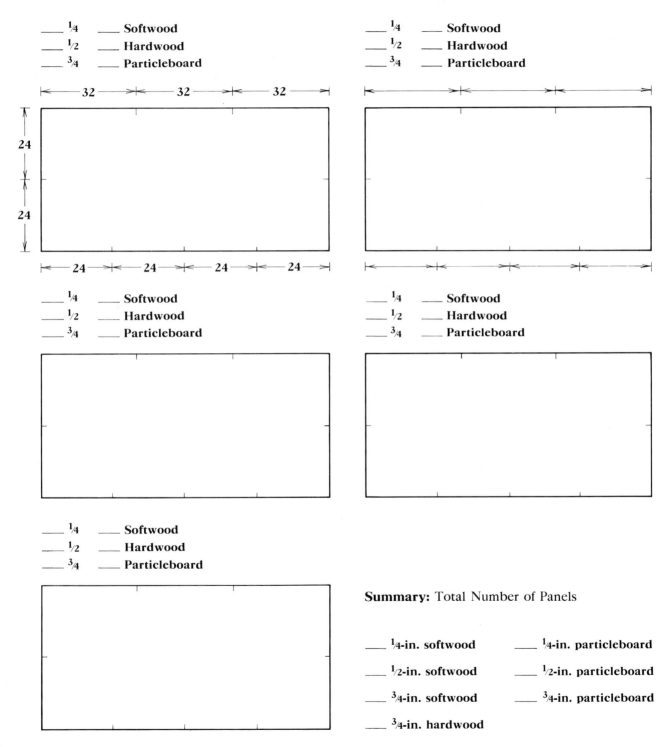

____ ¼   ____ Softwood
____ ½   ____ Hardwood
____ ¾   ____ Particleboard

____ ¼   ____ Softwood
____ ½   ____ Hardwood
____ ¾   ____ Particleboard

____ ¼   ____ Softwood
____ ½   ____ Hardwood
____ ¾   ____ Particleboard

____ ¼   ____ Softwood
____ ½   ____ Hardwood
____ ¾   ____ Particleboard

____ ¼   ____ Softwood
____ ½   ____ Hardwood
____ ¾   ____ Particleboard

Summary: Total Number of Panels

____ ¼-in. softwood   ____ ¼-in. particleboard

____ ½-in. softwood   ____ ½-in. particleboard

____ ¾-in. softwood   ____ ¾-in. particleboard

____ ¾-in. hardwood

Bibliography

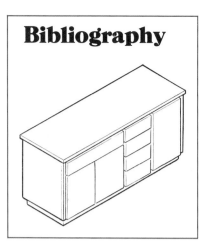

Architectural Woodwork Institute. **Architectural Woodwork Quality Standards and Guide Specifications.** Arlington, Va.: Architectural Woodwork Institute, 1973.

Specifies quality of materials, joinery, acceptable levels of sanding marks, etc., for three grades of cabinets (103 pages).

Feirer, John L. **Cabinetmaking and Millwork.** Rev. ed. New York: Scribners, 1977.

A fine text that touches lightly on most facets of woodworking, including kitchen cabinetmaking (928 pages).

Frid, Tage. **Tage Frid Teaches Woodworking—Joinery: Tools and Techniques.** Newtown, Conn.: The Taunton Press, 1979.

A craftsman's approach to a variety of joinery problems and the selection of power and hand tools. Includes a great many illustrations and photographs, which make the directions easy to understand and follow (224 pages).

Gibbia, S.W. **Wood Finishing and Refinishing.** Rev. ed. New York: Van Nostrand Reinhold, 1971.

Most of this book is devoted to special finishes for furniture, but there's a lot of information on preparing the wood, selecting materials and applying different finishes, which can be useful to kitchen cabinetmakers (271 pages).

Hammond, James J., et al. **Woodworking Technology.** Rev. ed. Bloomington, Ill.: McKnight Publishing Co., 1972.

A secondary-school text that covers the basics of wood and related materials, woodworking tools and basic woodworking processes (457 pages).

Hayward, Charles H. **Staining and Wood Polishing.** New York: Sterling Publishing Co., 1979.

Techniques for finishing floors, furniture and doors. Includes tips on choosing finishes and applying stains, fillers and finishes (214 pages).

Hoadley, R. Bruce. **Understanding Wood.** Newtown, Conn.: The Taunton Press, 1980.

A detailed but easily understood book that probes deeply into wood technology. It answers the serious woodworker's questions about everything from the growth of wood to the effects of moisture, machining and finishing (247 pages).

Holtrop, W.F. **Operation of Modern Woodworking Machines.** Rev. ed. Encino, Calif.: Glencoe Publishing Co., 1966.

An advanced woodworking text covering safety and the setup and operation of common woodworking machinery (176 pages).

Mattingly, C. Jean. "Remaking Your Own Kitchen." **Family Circle Great Ideas,** August 1981, pp. 22-25.

An informative article on kitchen design, dealing with basic kitchen shapes and kitchen layout.

The Reader's Digest Association. **Complete Do-it-yourself Manual.** Pleasantville, N.Y.: The Reader's Digest Association, 1973.

Detailed instructions on home maintenance and minor remodeling projects. Contains many drawings and photos (600 pages).

Sunset Editors. **Modern Kitchens.** Rev. ed. Menlo Park, Calif.: Lane Magazine & Book Co., 1965.

A good idea book, providing basic information on kitchen layout and work centers, as well as architect-designed floor plans (112 pages) *Out of print.*

Sunset Editors. **Tile: Remodeling.** Menlo Park, Calif.: Lane Publishing Co., 1978.

Good design ideas using wood, vinyl and ceramic tile. Also includes a substantial amount of how-to instruction (80 pages).

U.S. Department of Commerce, National Bureau of Standards. **Voluntary Product Standard PS 51-71: Hardwood and Decorative Plywood.** Washington, D.C.: U.S. Government Printing Office, 1972.

Contains the requirements for different grades of hardwood plywood, including wood species, veneer grading, glue bond, panel construction, moisture content, sanding and finishing. Also includes a glossary of trade terms (18 pages).

Index

Editor: Laura Cehanowicz Tringali
Designer: Roger Barnes
Layout: Lee Hochgraf Hov
Assistant Editor: Roger Holmes
Copy Editor: Deborah Cannarella
Illustrations: Heather Brine Lambert, Lee Hochgraf Hov
Manager of Production Services: Gary Mancini
Production Manager: Mary Galpin
Typesetter: Nancy-Lou Knapp
Darkroom: Annette Hilty, Deborah Mason, Jay Smith

Typeface: Caslon Modified 9½ point
Paper: Sterling Web Matte, 80 lb., Neutral pH
Printer: R.R. Donnelley & Sons, Willard, Ohio